INFORMATION TECHNOLOGY IN 21ST CENTURY

INFORMATION TECHNOLOGY IN 21ST CENTURY

(In 9 Volumes)

TRENDS OF CYBERIA

Challenges of the Future

(Volume 3)

PROF. RAMESH CHANDRA

Vice-Chancellor, Bundelkhand University, Jhansi (U.P.)

Publication

KALPAZ PUBLICATIONS

DELHI–110052

INFORMATION TECHNOLOGY IN 21ST CENTURY
Trends of Cyberia: Challenges of the Future
(Information Technolgy)

Rs. 8000 (Set)
Rs. 900 (each volume)

ISBN: 81-7835-158-7 (Set)
ISBN: 81-7835-161 7 (Vol. 3)

Published in 2003 in India by
Kalpaz Publications
C-30, Satyawati Nagar
Delhi-110052
E-mail: kalpaz@hotmail.com

Laser Typesetting at: A.S. Printers
Printed at: Chawla Offset Printers, Delhi

Preface

From time immemorial man used certain signals to amplify the information such as bonfires, semaphores, drumbeats, etc. All served as signals of some kind of information. Later it became an accepted fact that information is the vital resource in developmental activities. The twentieth century witnessed an exciting and exhaustive explosion in the arena of information amplification. The invention of computers and internet introduced dramatic change in the arena of information dissemination.

The global telecommunication network that forms the platform for internet brings the ability to disseminate information on a massive scale. Whilst this features creating wonderful opportunities in many ways, it poses a larger number of problems in terms of intellectual property rights. These intellectual property rights include patents, copyrights, trade secrets, trademarks, etc. The cyber intellectual property rights also include expression of ideas and inventions with commercial goodwill.

The cyberspace witnesses so many controversial issues such as the piracy of intellectual property. Crimes against intellectual property include piracy and theft. The illegal acquisition and distribution of copyright materials including electronic and print form, compact discs, software stored in computer files and distributed on discs, etc., come under the wing of piracy.

The legal protection of computer software and other intellectual property of cyberspace has become a matter of very substantial concern following the population explosion of personal computers and the internet connections. The patents are directed to protect creative innovations from piracy. The policy behind patent protection is to promote the disclosure and availability to the public of innovative devices and methods. The essence of protection provided under patent laws is the right to exclude others from making, using and selling the innovation covered by the patent for a particular period of time, from the date the patent was issued.

This book attempts to analyse the burning issues of cyberspace and find out the proper legal framework to regulate them. Written in a simple and effective style, it is designed to provide proper guidance to computer professionals, academics, researchers, students, investigative officers and also for the lay public, who have little knowledge of cyberspace.

Editor

Contents

1

Introduction

The internet has dramatically changed the world. An estimated 377 million individuals globally are now online. They are using the net to read news, talk to friends, buy goods, listen to music and for countless other activities. A significant number of people are using the internet to buy goods and services. As diverse networks of computers, telephones, television, cable and satellite merge, most activities in the developed world will be connected to online technology.

A Forrester research survey estimates that US business to consumer internet sales will reach US$108 billion by 2002. When asked about their worries regarding online shopping, consumers have ranked invasion of privacy as a top concern. An American Express survey of 11,000 consumers in 10 countries found that 79 percent cited privacy and security as a major concern in relation to online shopping. This fear is turning many consumers away from using electronic commerce because they are concerned about the potential abuse of their personal information by electronic commerce companies.

A survey by the US National Consumer League found that privacy was one of consumers' highest concerns. Fifty seven percent of the respondents said that they had not bought anything online in the last 12 months because they were worried that either their credit card number or their personal information would be abused. Other consumers reported that they provide false information to protect themselves. Forrester research estimates that electronic-commerce sales were reduced by $2.8 billion in 1999 because of privacy concerns.

While the technologies are developing at breakneck speed, the policies governing their use and the traditional protections that consumers have enjoyed for over a generation have lagged behind. In addition, new issues, such as defining jurisdiction and law in a world where transactions can easily occur between individuals in different countries and on different continents urgently need to be addressed. Some technology is emerging to provide protection for consumers but the scope is limited. Even more confusing for consumers is the fact that frequently, privacy-invasive technology that actually encourages capturing of data is misleadingly promoted as protecting privacy.

The Consumers International coordinated a study Consumers@shopping: an international comparative study of electronic commerce, published by Consumers International in September 1999, examined what happened when consumers bought a range of products over the internet. The aim was to find out how easy it was to shop on the internet, to identify problem areas, and to pinpoint good and bad practice. The shopping for this project was carried out in late 1998 and early 1999, and involved purchasing items both at home and abroad.

A range of problems was identified. These included companies that provided inadequate information to the consumer; sent goods that arrived late or did not turn up at all; and delayed refunds. One primary area targeted for criticism in the 1999 report was the sites' approach to data protection and privacy. Whilst almost all sites demanded certain pieces of personal information, only one in five explained to the consumer what use was made of this information. Most customers would expect to provide a minimum amount of information when buying something over the internet, but consumers do not necessarily want that information collected unless it is essential to the transaction. In particular, consumers do not want the information used for any purpose unrelated to the specific purchase they currently are conducting. The findings of Consumers@shopping indicated a great deal of interest in the privacy aspect of electronic commerce, and demonstrated a clear need for more detailed research.

Privacy Issues

Privacy is recognised as a fundamental human right in the Universal Declaration of Human Rights, adopted by the United Nations in 1948, and other international treaties. The range of issues that fall under the name of privacy is quite broad. These include secret communications and papers, protection of home and family, and bodily integrity. In electronic commerce, the protection of privacy concerns the setting of rules and limits on the collection, handling, and use of personal information that is gathered by companies and other organisations as part of the interaction between a consumer and those companies. This is commonly referred to as "data protection". Interest in data protection began in the 1960s with the increased use of computers in society.

The collection and use of personal information by powerful computer systems prompted demands for specific rules governing the collection and handling of personal information. Electronic commerce raises new concerns about privacy because the scope and detail of personal information collected about consumers is far greater than is usually collected in the off-line world. The internet environment allows businesses to collect, analyse and use more information about customers, and with more ease and efficiency than ever before.

The possibilities for storing, comparing, and linking information to build up a detailed picture of a customer's interests are huge. There have always been concerns over the way businesses use personal information, but the ease with which they can collect and manipulate that information on the internet makes the scale of the problem much larger. To add to the complexity of the situation, the internet has the potential for opening up markets – both for shopping and information-gathering – in other countries, which have widely diverse laws governing data protection. There are important differences between how information is collected on customers who shop online versus those who shop the old-fashioned way – on the high street and in the malls.

Two of the most important differences are that most online companies keep track of users' visits and purchases. Unlike most consumer transactions off-line, detailed information is collected about individuals' actions even if they do not purchase anything. Secondly the consumer's name, address and perhaps even phone number – and often additional details as well – are collected for virtually every purchase as a condition of payment by credit card or for shipping purposes.

The computers that log all activities on their systems routinely capture all these particulars. The information ranges from the trivial to the most sensitive. In a typical electronic commerce transaction, this information would include not just the record of the items actually purchased but a list of all other others that were viewed.

Companies also often collect information from consumers in exchange for a free service, such. Background as news searches, free email and stock portfolios. In many cases, users are not informed that the information is being collected. Not surprisingly, however, those customer details are frequently fodder for targeting advertising. Companies such as Netzero offer free net access in exchange for monitoring their users' activities for advertisers.

Web sites known as "portals" offer personalised pages where a user can set up a free account to get selected news or stock quotes or chat with other users once they register and provide their names, addresses and interests. A key concept in online marketing is personalisation. This is the belief that marketers can collect enough information about consumers to determine their desires for goods and to target specific advertising or other services at them.

The perceived value of this information is what makes many of these dot.com companies worth so much on the stock market. The companies then sell, trade or share that information among third party companies without the consumer's express knowledge or consent.

Internet security

Many web sites that retain personal information are poorly secured against accidental releases or deliberate attempts to penetrate computer systems for fraudulent purposes. At least one major security flaw in common software used by consumers and consumer-oriented businesses is discovered every week. It is common to have security breaches that result in the disclosure of personal information or financial records. Many electronic commerce companies respond to concerns about security by stating that they are using encryption to scramble the communications between the user and the server – to prevent a third party from eavesdropping – when the user is providing sensitive information.

However, this protection is largely illusory. That information is highly vulnerable once it is collected and included on online databases. Leaks of personal and credit card information occur daily, many involving hundreds of thousands of records. Thousands of customers of CD universe had to replace their credit cards after the database was stolen and offered for sale on the internet.

In August 2000, Kaiser Permanente, a top US health insurer, admitted that it had compromised the confidentiality and privacy of its members when it sent over 800 email messages, many containing sensitive information, to the wrong members. In many cases, the consumer is not even aware that the information is on the net. Here are just two frightening examples: in Michigan, health information, including names, social security numbers and diagnostic codes of thousands of patients, was placed on the internet by the University of Michigan health care system and was publicly available for months. The US Social Security administration made their retirement database available on the internet in 1997 without any prior consultation.

Spam

Unsolicited commercial email, commonly known as "spam," is a major nuisance. Each day, millions of unsolicited electronic mails are sent to consumers. The Gartner Group estimates that 90% of all internet users receive one item of spam at least weekly and half receive six or more each week. It is estimated that the average consumer will receive 1,600 spam messages each year by 2005. Spam is an example of the failure to apply fair information practices. Addresses are purchased from electronic commerce companies and harvested secretly from web pages, discussion groups, and web chats. Consumer consent is not asked before the address is collected, used or transferred. Consumers have few options for reducing this problem. Once a consumer's email address is on a list, it is difficult to remove. Many spam messages do not have real return addresses. Even if there is a real address, many spammers take return messages to create new lists of verified email addresses that they can sell for a greater amount. It is also difficult to use technical measures to filter out unwanted messages, since they come from thousands of different addresses.

Much of the spam now arrives with misleading subjects such as "regarding your message", to encourage consumers to read the email. Spam clutters up consumers' email boxes and makes it difficult to find important email. Many consumers are forced to change their email addresses and services to avoid spam. Some stop using the internet altogether because they are tired of receiving so much junk.

Spam also costs the consumer money. In many areas around the world, the consumer must pay per minute or download charges to either the telephone company or the internet service provider. In addition, many internet service providers have to expend extensive resources hiring staff and buying additional equipment to deal with the flood of electronic mail they receive – and that cost is passed on to their customers. America Online (AOL) estimates that one-third of incoming mail to its servers – between 10 and 24 million messages each day – is spam. An industry association estimated in 1999 that $2 of each customer's bill could be traced to spam-related costs. Marketers can also use spam to track user activities.

Spam that is sent in html form and read by users of AOL or many other common email programs can send messages to advertising networks such as DoubleClick, linking consumers' email addresses with their cookies.Most of the manufacturers suppressed the number after a consumer boycott was announced, and Intel announced in 2000 that it is dropping the serial number in future chips. Soon after, several companies, including Microsoft and RealAudio, were discovered using the internal networking number found in most computers as another identifier. The Internet Engineering Task Force has developed specifications for the next version of the Internet's underlying protocols called IPv6 that will assign a unique permanent ID number to every device hooked into the net, which could one day include common household devices such as refrigerators and VCRs.

The growing use of wireless devices also raises serious concerns. Several US cellular phone providers disclose the user's phone number as well as their Internet address when a customer uses their phone to access the Internet. Growing numbers of programmes and devices exist that secretly monitor the activities of the user and send information back to the company that created it. In some cases, the software sends back a unique identifier. In others, such as with RealPlayer, the software sends a unique identifier and detailed information on the music that the user was listening to. Recently, readers of Wired, Forbes and other magazines were sent a free plug-in bar code scanner called the CueCat. Using the device, users can visit websites by reading bar codes in magazines and newspapers or that are encoded into television shows or ads. At the same time, the devices contain a unique ID number and maintain a detailed database of the users' activities.

When hobbyists starting developing their own software that deleted the ID number and bypassed the corporate database, the companies' lawyers threatened them with violating intellectual property. The convergence of communications networks, computers and mass media into an interactive network combining television and the Internet is the next progression of the technology currently being developed. Slowly, intelligent cable TV boxes, which can use broadband and interactive cable systems, are being deployed in many jurisdictions around the world. The new systems are being designed, like their Internet predecessors, to track every activity of users as they surf the net through the boxes. They also are being designed to track the shows and commercials users watch and to use that information to tailor advertising for the greatest effect.

The industry calls this "T-Commerce" for Television Commerce. Millions of consumers are expected to be using these in just the next few years, and the ad revenue to justify the new expensive boxes is expected to hit $5 billion by 2004. Media titan Rupert Murdoch said of the box in a recent NewsCorp annual report, "It will tell us not only who the customers are, but what they buy, what they watch, what they read and what they want." Unlike personal computers that give users control over their actions and choices, the new TV systems are generally based on a sealed "black box" controlled by the company that gives the user little or no control. In the WebTV box, users are not able to refuse cookies or delete them afterwards. The systems are closed and it is difficult, if not impossible, for even advanced users to identify what the system is doing. It will also prevent users from being able to use their own software. Meanwhile, there are other companies that have developed devices that will automatically record television shows for viewers and make recommendations for new shows based on viewers' previous behaviour. These systems also send some information on the viewers' habits back to the central offices. In the future, advertisers plan to combine marketing with mobile phone location so that marketers will be able to page or message customers on their phones to alert them to shopping opportunities – as they are passing selected restaurants, for example, or a sporting goods store.

Privacy laws

More recently, countries began adopting laws protecting citizens from the publication of their personal information. France prohibited the publication of private facts and set stiff fines for violators in 1858. The Norwegian criminal code prohibited the publication of information relating to "personal or domestic affairs" in 1889. In 1890, American lawyers Samuel Warren and Louis Brandeis wrote a seminal piece on the right to privacy as a tort action, describing privacy as "the right to be left alone."

Following the publication, this concept of the privacy tort was gradually picked up across the US as part of the common law. The modern privacy benchmark at an international level can be found in the 1948 Universal Declaration of Human Rights, which specifically protects territorial and communications privacy. It also recognises that individuals have a right to legal protections against invasions of their privacy. Interest in the right of privacy increased in the 1960s and 1970s with the advent of information technology. The surveillance potential of powerful computer systems prompted demands for specific rules governing the collection and handling of personal information. The genesis of modern legislation in this area can be traced to the first data protection law in the world enacted in the Land of Hesse in Germany in 1970. National laws in Sweden (1973), the United States (1974), Germany (1977), and France (1978) followed this. Today, over 30 countries have comprehensive laws governing the processing and use of personal information.

A major milestone was the European Union's adoption of data protection laws in 1995 and 1997, to harmonise laws throughout the EU in order to ensure consistent levels of protections for citizens, and to allow for the free flow of personal information throughout the EU. The Directives set a baseline common level of privacy which not only reinforce current data protection law, but extended it to establish a range of new rights. The 1995 Data Protection Directive set a benchmark for national law for processing personal information in electronic and manual files.

The 1997 Telecommunications Directive established specific protections covering telephone, digital television, mobile networks and other telecommunications systems. In July 2000, the European Commission, issued a proposal for a new directive on "the processing of personal data and the protection of privacy in the electronic communications sector. " It will replace the existing 1997 Telecommunications Directive by extending the existing protections for an individual's "telecommunications" to a broader, more technology-neutral category of "electronic communications." These new provisions would, for example, ensure the protection of all information ("traffic") transmitted across the Internet, prohibit unsolicited commercial marketing by e-mail (spam) without opt-in consent, and protect mobile phone users from precise location tracking and surveillance. The directive also gives subscribers to all electronic communications services (such as GSM and e-mail) the right to chose whether they are listed in a public directory. In all of the EU efforts, enforceability is a key concept.

The EU is concerned that data subjects have rights that are enshrined in explicit rules, and that they can go to a person or an authority empowered to act on their behalf. Every EU country has a Data Protection Commissioner or agency that enforces the rules. It is expected that the countries with which Europe does business will need to provide a similar level of oversight. The Directive imposes an obligation on Member States to ensure that the personal information relating to European citizens has the same level of protection when it is exported to, and processed in, countries outside the EU. Many countries outside the EU have adopted similar laws. This is especially common in Central and Eastern Europe where the countries are attempting to join the EU and the Council of Europe.

Many countries in the Western Hemisphere are also moving forward. In Canada, the Federal Parliament approved Bill C-6, the Personal Information Protection and Electronic Documents Act in April 2000. The Act adopts the Canadian Standards Association's International Privacy Code into law for enterprises that process personal information "in the course of a commercial activity," and for federally regulated employers with respect to their employees. In three years, the Act will cover provincially regulated sectors unless the province enacts "substantially similar" laws, such as Quebéc's law. Laws based on the EU Directives have also been approved in Chile and Argentina. In Asia, Hong Kong and Taiwan have already adopted laws and nearly a dozen other countries are actively considering new laws on data protection.

Some countries, such as the United States, have avoided enacting general data protection rules in favour of laws governing specific areas such as medical or financial records. In such cases, enforcement is achieved through a range of mechanisms. A major drawback with this approach is that it requires that new legislation be introduced with each new technology, so protections frequently lag behind. The lack of legal protections for medical and genetic information in the US is a striking example of its limitations. There is also the problem of a lack of an oversight agency. In many countries, sectoral laws are used to complement comprehensive legislation by providing more detailed protections for certain categories of information, such as telecommunications, police files or consumer credit records. Other countries such as South Korea and Mexico have adopted specific laws on electronic commerce that also protect privacy.

Another possible method for protecting privacy is through industry self-regulation, in which companies and industry bodies establish codes of practice and engage in self-policing. Self-regulation has different meanings in the US and Europe. In the US, which lacks a comprehensive privacy protection law, industry is not required to follow any minimal standards and there is little evidence that the aims of the codes are regularly fulfilled. There is also a serious problem with enforcement. In Europe, there is discussion of self-regulation, but in the EU context, self-regulation usually means that industry develops codes based on the standards in the national data protection laws and enforcement is ensured by the national data protection agencies. In an effort to promote self-regulation, industry is focusing on adopting website privacy policies that provide some information to consumers on what details are collected and how they are used and disclosed. Most major e-commerce sites in the United States have adopted these policies. Consumers have found numerous problems with these policies.

Of primary concern is that in an unregulated environment such as the United States, there is no minimum standard for the policy. Many of the privacy policies. simply state that they are collecting a great deal of information about users and that they are planning to use that information for unknown purposes at their discretion and disclose that information to an unknown number of outside organisations for unknown reasons. A number of surveys by the US Federal Trade Commission and independent groups such as EPIC, in addition to this study by Consumers International, have found that most privacy policies do not adequately protect privacy. Because there is no legal framework, the privacy policies can be changed at will by the company. Bookseller Amazon.com recently changed its policy from promising never to sell the personal information of its customers to notifying users that it may do at some point in the future. DoubleClick went from offering a semi-anonymous system to an attempt to merge their online records with personal information from offline.

Problems also arise when the legal status of a company changes. If a company goes bankrupt or is bought by another company, the privacy protections of the policy are in doubt. The information can also be placed in the public record because it is frequently the only asset of the company. When Living.com filed for bankruptcy, the trustee placed the names and addresses of thousands of customers on the web. Finally, enforcement of privacy policies in countries without laws such as the United States is limited. At best, the consumer can ask the Federal Trade Commission or state Attorney General to enforce the promises. Not surprisingly, this works very infrequently. Tools are available that can protect the privacy of users in many cases. These technologies are known as "Privacy Enhancing Technologies" (PETs) and include anonymous web browsers, remailers and encryption. The European Commission in 1998 looked as some PETs and stated that the tools would not replace a legal framework but could be used to compliment existing laws. Encryption has become the most important tool for protection against surveillance. A message is scrambled so that only the intended recipient will be able to unscramble, and subsequently read the contents. Pretty Good Privacy (PGP) is the best-known encryption program and has hundreds of thousands of users, including human rights groups. An open source program called GNU Privacy Guard is being developed as a free replacement that will allow anyone to view the full source of the system to ensure that it does not allow for secret surveillance. "Anonymous remailers" strip identifying information from e-mails and can stop traffic analysis. They have generated opposition from police and intelligence services.

In Finland, a popular anonymous remailer had to be shut down due to legal challenges that forced the operator to reveal the name of one of the users. More advanced tools that merge the functions of anonymous remailers and encryption have also been developed. The Mixmaster anonymous remailers used encryption links between anonymous remailers to hide the identity of the original sender by sending the message randomly through a series of remailers before delivering it to the final destination. Another useful tool allows consumers to browse anonymously. Many of these services also prevent cookies, or applications that can be used to spy on the consumer from being placed on the consumer's computer. The most sophisticated ones, such as Freedom.net, provide a fully encrypted link between the user and secure servers run by the company to prevent wiretapping, and encrypted headers so that users can receive email and browse the Internet without even the company knowing who is using the system. Users should be aware that not all tools are effective at protecting privacy. A major limitation is that almost none of the tools address the protection of privacy once the information is collected.

Encryption is useful for ensuing that personal information is protected in transit but this says nothing about how the information is used by the companies once it collected. Industry also offers many tools that are not privacy-protective. Many of these systems, such as Microsoft's Passport and the World Wide Web Consortium's (W3C) Platform for Privacy Preferences (P3P), are designed more to facilitate data sharing than to protect users. They are also frequently used by US industry as justification for not passing laws. Marketing hype frequently promotes tools as privacy protective that have nothing to do with privacy. American Express announced in October 2000 its Private Payments program, which would allow for the creation of one-time credit card numbers for online purchases.

Consumers International's main objective in coordinating this survey was to compare the experience of consumers in the United States (US) and the European Union (EU) because there are major differences in approaches to regulation. Privacy practices are voluntary and business-led in the US. In the EU, many key consumer rights are enshrined both in EU and national legislation. Consumer organisations have expressed concern that EU consumers could be vulnerable to abuse of their personal data when buying from the US or using US-based websites. Following the approval of the EU Data Protection Directive, many large American companies worried that they would be cut off from data flows from European countries because of the lack of laws protecting privacy in the US. The US government and industry strongly lobbied the EU and member countries to find the US system adequate. In 1998, the US began negotiating a safe harbour agreement with the EU in order to ensure the continued trans-border flow of personal data.

Negotiations on the drafting of the principles lasted nearly two years and were the subject of bitter criticism by privacy and consumer advocates and the European Parliament. In July 2000, despite the criticisms, the Commission approved the safe harbour agreement. Under safe harbour, US companies can voluntarily self-certify to adhere to a set of privacy principles loosely based on the fair information practices developed by the US Department of Commerce and the European Commission. These companies could then continue to receive personal data from the European Union. US companies have been able to join safe harbour from November 2000. However take-up has been remarkably slow, with only one company reportedly joining up as of early December 2000. There is an open-ended grace period for US signatory companies to implement the principles. The Commission promised to re-open negotiations on the arrangement if the remedies available to European citizens prove inadequate. There are many concerns that the proposal will not adequately protect consumers. A major weakness of the agreement is enforcement. The agreement rests on a self-regulatory system, whereby companies merely promise not to violate their declared privacy practices. There is little enforcement or systematic review of compliance.

Individual consumers have no right to appeal or right to compensation for privacy infringements. The agreement will only apply to companies overseen by the Federal Trade Commission and Department of

Transportation and special exceptions are granted for public record information protected by EU law. It does not apply to internet or electronic commerce unless a European electronic commerce company transfers information about its customers to a US company that has signed up to the agreement.

2

Consumer Culture

Today, we rededicate ourselves to continuing to work for social and economic justice and to work with other public interest groups because we are all consumers and we are all citizens. The dramatic changes that have taken place over the last decades have created great challenges for us. They have also inspired us to develop the policies and strategies that can help bring social and economic justice to all the peoples of the world. The essential starting point for Consumers International's policies is the eight basic rights of consumers.

The World Consumer Congress held in Africa, draw particular attention to the problems of establishing these rights and ensuring that the processes of globalisation contribute to social justice as well as economic development across the continent. We call on international bodies and governments to establish and implement plans and programmes recognising the special needs of Africa. Measures should be taken to promote democracy and the respect of human rights, including economic, social, cultural, civil and political rights, to fight corruption, improve governance, reduce the burden of debt and promote a healthy and sustainable environment. Consumer policy can contribute to poverty eradication, efficient markets, good governance and the promotion of human rights.

All governments should actively pursue the three pillars of consumer policy – consumer legislation and regulations, consumer representation and the empowerment of individual consumers. The United Nation's Guidelines for Consumer Protection and Consumers International's Model Laws provide guidelines for some of the necessary elements of consumer policy. All countries should have comprehensive consumer protection legislation, effectively implemented and including means to ensure access to justice. Specific measures are needed to protect consumers from hazardous products and technologies. Consumers International, working with its members, should encourage the introduction of appropriate legislation and governments should hold conferences on consumer protection in accordance with ECOSOC Resolution 1990/85.

Consumers International and its members should place special emphasis on the needs and difficulties of vulnerable and disadvantaged consumers, especially where these are poorer consumers, women, children, older people, indigenous people and people with disabilities.

Consumers International recognises that many of today's consumption patterns cannot be sustained without risk of exhausting the world's natural resources and of long-term and perhaps irreversible damage to the environment. Continued economic development is essential to meet human needs. However, strategies must be found to improve the quality of life for consumers while preserving the natural environment and ensuring equitable distribution of the world's resources. Consumer organisations can play an important role in initiating and advocating change in consumption patterns, and have the means to provide consumers with information that allows them to make informed choices. They should also encourage governments and business to adopt policies and methods that will promote sustainable consumption, in accordance with the new sections of the UN Guidelines on Consumer Protection, adopted in 1999.

Business, governments and, where appropriate, international agencies should adopt plans of action to promote environmental protection and sustainable development, and specifically should:

- co-operate in the vital task of eradicating poverty as this is an indispensable requirement for establishing sustainable consumption;
- develop and apply technologies and methods that are environmentally sustainable for both poor and affluent consumers;
- work toward mandatory targets for major, sustainable reductions in greenhouse gas emissions;
- reduce wasteful energy production and consumption patterns and promote a supply of sustainable alternative energy sources;
- promote urban transport systems and policies, and forms of urban development, that minimise dependence on personal motor vehicles where they exacerbate pollution levels;
- review existing eco-labels and their demands critically, and reduce the number in use to a few which are internationally recognised and reliable;

— promote safe, efficient, ozone-protective and low-cost alternatives to CFCs, HFCs and HCFCs;

— promote biodiversity, natural ecosystems and water supplies, and promote sustainable agriculture and forestry practices and policies;

— promote investment in renewable resources and policies which influence demand.

Consumers International and its members are encouraged to build alliances with like-minded bodies and to lobby governments and international agencies to raise the level of public debate and awareness, to support policies and influence public opinion in order to:

— promote the steps above and others that reduce wasteful use of resources and prevent damage to the environment;

— reduce levels of resource use by developed countries, and by over-consuming sectors in developing countries;

— support environmental protection and standards while ensuring that these are not abused as trade barriers;

— ensure that animal protection measures are taken into account provided that these are not abused as trade barriers;

— ensure that consumers have sound information and education on the environmental impacts of their buying decisions and lifestyle choices;

— formulate a clear policy on the management of durability features in their testing and reporting activities, and live up to these policies in practice;

— generate public support for government policies described above;

— raise consumer awareness of production and marketing practices that promote expectations and lifestyles not consistent with sound environmental policies.

The daily lives of consumers across the world are directly affected by the actions of governments and international institutions in regulating and liberalising trade, investment and the practices of international business. Speculative financial flows, regional and multilateral trade liberalisation, and corporate mergers and acquisitions are of particular concern. Consumers International and its members should seek to ensure that the interests and rights of consumers are recognised and protected in international trade and economic agreements.

Governments and international agencies should:

— ensure that trade and economic policies are formed with the involvement of, and take into account the interests of, all stakeholders, including consumers;

— ensure that all governments have the capacity to represent and negotiate on behalf of their people;

— cancel the debt of least developed countries;

— encourage the World Trade Organisation (WTO) and other such bodies to operate in an open and accessible manner and establish regular and effective consultation with consumer groups and other NGOs;

— reduce tariff and non-tariff trade barriers which have a negative impact on consumers and end 'voluntary' agreements which escape international trade rules;

- reform protectionist agricultural policies which produce expensive surpluses dumped on world markets;
- reassess the link between the Agreement on Trade Related Intellectual Property (TRIPs) and global agreements to protect biodiversity, recognising that consumers' rights come before those of business in the field of access to medicines, patenting life forms, biotechnology and biodiversity and that the rights of farmers in the developing world should be protected;
- through international co-operation, examine the effects of the global movement of capital on people and their nation states and seek to curb any negative effects of such movements which create further marginalisation and inequality;
- introduce legislation to set standards which transnational corporations (TNCs) must observe and agree a framework for monitoring TNC behaviour.

Business should:

- observe existing voluntary codes of conduct, such as the Organisation for Economic Co-operation and Development (OECD) Guidelines for Multinational Enterprises, the Code of Ethics on the International Trade in Chemicals, relevant articles of Agenda 21, and the UN Guidelines on Consumer Protection;
- engage with consumer organisations with a view to improving the transparency of business operations and understanding better local consumer needs.

Consumers International and its members should:

- research the impact of trade and economic liberalisation on the daily lives of consumers including environmental and social effects and inequality;

— work with international organisations as a way to influence and advise governments and others on consumer policies and priorities;

— promote the use of competition policy which enhances consumer welfare nationally;

— build the capacity of consumer organisations to influence national trade and competition policies.

Changes in the management and regulation of public utilities — water, electricity, gas and telecommunications —and the technologies which they use, directly affect the price, quality and reliability of these services and access to them, and thus the most fundamental rights of consumers. The consumer interest should be the overriding concern in planning the future of these services, including decisions about their privatisation. Essential requirements are: universal access, including if necessary special programmes to address the needs of poor consumers; accurate invoicing and forms of payment; formal published standards to ensure quality, durability and safety; the promotion of energy conservation; comprehensive and fair procedures for complaints and claims; and independent regulation supported by effective legal powers.

The first priority of all governments should be to make safe and affordable water available to all consumers. Privatisation should not be regarded as necessary. In some circumstances, it may be appropriate, but this is unlikely to be the case where effective consumer protection legislation and institutions are not in place. Where privatisation is being considered, governments should ensure that the local community's views are properly considered to safeguard their interests, and that alternatives are thoroughly studied. Consumer organisations should have an active role in privatisation debates, which must be transparent and include public access to relevant documents.

Consumer education is essential to provide the skills and knowledge to empower consumers and enable them to use their resources effectively and increase their awareness of their wider role in society.Consumer education addresses not only problems of consumers individually but also of sustainable consumption, social justice, human rights, ethical values and poverty eradication. Consumer education contributes towards the formation of a participative, critical and competent citizenship.

All governments should be urged to incorporate consumer education as a mandatory part of the basic school curriculum. Consumers International and its members should promote the importance of consumer education programmes both to governments and to international agencies, and develop greater contacts with the media and use it for implementing programmes. International co-operation provides a valuable means of increasing the expertise and information available to consumer organisations and educators. Consumers International and its members should continue to support consumer education networks and explore the possibility of creating and maintaining:

— a clearinghouse of consumer education material taking into account the importance of multilingual publications;

— a training centre based in a developing country for consumer activists and officials;

— a worldwide agreement with UNESCO and with institutions specialising in consumer education to promote it in as many countries as possible.

International rules and standards have an important impact on the safe design, performance and fitness for purpose of products and services, and hence provide vital safeguards and protection for consumers. These rules and standards are made by a number of bodies. Standards must be developed taking into account actual use by consumers, the range of consumers exposed to the product and different cultural and climatic needs of consumers in different regions. Governments should only undertake harmonisation of standards where there is a clear benefit for consumers and where it is understood that the standards setting process must respect democratic values. Consumers International and its members should play an active role in standardisation. They should participate in the development of Consumers International policies and in technical committees preparing national and international standards of consumer interest. They should act in co-operation with other international bodies representing consumers. All bodies responsible for standard setting should actively seek and facilitate the participation of consumer representatives in their work.

Consumers International and its members should:

— set up discussion networks on international standardisation;

— increase their work on the Codex Alimentarius, which has become a focus for setting global food standards following trade liberalisation and the establishment of the WTO;

— liaise closely with the International Organisation for Standardisation's consumer body (ISO/COPOLCO) and with other appropriate international and regional bodies, with the aim of achieving consumer representation on standards committees dealing with agreed priority issues for consumers;

— seek to ensure that all standards bodies operate in a transparent manner and develop standards by a clearly understood consensus process involving consumers.

Consumers International and its members encourage governments, the Codex Alimentarius Commission, FAO and WHO and other standards organisations, as appropriate, to:

— set up and/or support consumer participation in National Standards Bodies and their committees;

— assure adequate representation of the consumer interest and provide funds to enable consumer organisations to participate in appropriate standards work including relevant national, sub-regional and regional workshops, seminars and meetings;

— ensure democratic and transparent processes in standards making and the full participation of all countries;

— set up and/or support National Codex Committees with active consumer participation;

— increase public awareness and understanding of the Codex and standards process.

Consumers International should seek to stimulate research and testing activities in different regions through sharing experiences between testing organisations and newer groups, through training programmes and through structured regional testing programmes. There should be at least one organisation in each region that can act as a focus for co-ordinating testing expertise.

The development of information technology and publishing and broadcast media provide many opportunities for empowering consumers and aiding the work of consumer organisations.For these benefits to be exploited, both access and appropriate regulation need to be assured. Access needs particular attention to ensure that information technology does not promote the marginalisation of disadvantaged consumers and countries.

Consumers International and its members should seek to ensure that consumer interests are effectively represented at agencies dealing with international information technology and media policies - particularly in relation to issues of privacy, the regulation of advertising and services which cross national frontiers, and the regulation of interactive services. Changes in the media sector should also be monitored and policies sought which ensure diversity of ownership.

Effective consumer protection should be established for transactions made via the internet; these should be at least as effective and reliable as consumer protection for traditional transactions. Access, privacy, security, dispute resolution, and applicable laws and jurisdiction for the internet and electronic commerce should be included in any legal standard.

Where consumer rights depend on adherence to voluntary best practice guidelines, consumers need to be able to recognise internet shops and other services that offer high standards of consumer protection. The development of an internationally-recognised certification or labelling scheme should be supported. An internationally-recognised third-party redress mechanism should be developed. The feasibility of a worldwide computerised consumer database, information programmes which might be shared by consumer organisations, and an information technology guidance service for consumer organisation, should be assessed.

3

Security in Cyberspace

Because the Internet is a global network, international issues may arise in many cases; even a domestic investigation may involve a computer system, data, witness or subject located in a foreign jurisdiction. The United States maintains approximately 40 bilateral mutual legal assistance treaty relationships and many other relationships pursuant to letters rogatory or other longstanding means of cooperation.

While cooperation with respect to computer and electronic evidence is, under further development internationally, these treaty structures and ongoing relationships continue to provide the legal and practical means by which the United States both seeks and provides legal assistance. When agents learn prior to a search that some of all of the data to be searched is located in a foreign jurisdiction, they should seek advice from the Office of International Affairs as to the need for and appropriate means to seek assistance from that country. When immediate international assistance is required, the international network of 24-hour Points of

Contact established by the High-tech Crime Subgroup of the G-8 countries can provide assistance, such as preserving data and assisting in real-time tracing of cross-border communications. The Critical Challenges from International High-Tech and Computer-Related Crime at the Millennium. The network is available twenty-four hours a day to respond to urgent requests for assistance in international high-tech crime investigations, or cases involving electronic evidence. The membership currently includes Australia, Brazil, Canada, Denmark, Finland, France, Germany, Italy, Japan, Republic of Korea, Luxembourg, Russia, Spain, Sweden, United Kingdom, and the United States, and continues to grow. CCIPS also has computer crime law enforcement contacts in countries beyond members of the network; agents and prosecutors can call CCIPS for assistance.

When agents have reason to believe that a search may result in a seizure of materials relating to First Amendment activities such as publishing or posting materials on the World Wide Web, they must consider the effect of the Privacy Protection Act ('PPA'). Every federal computer search that implicates the PPA must be approved by the Deputy Assistant Attorney General of the Criminal Division, coordinated through CCIPS. Under the Privacy Protection Act ('PPA'), law enforcement must take special steps when planning a search that agents have reason to believe may result in the seizure of certain First Amendment materials. Federal law enforcement searches that implicate the PPA must be pre-approved by the Justice Department in Washington, D.C. The Computer Crime and Intellectual Property Section serves as the contact point for all such searches involving computers, and should be contacted directly.

Before the Supreme Court decided Warden v. Hayden, law enforcement officers could not obtain search warrants to search for and seize 'mere evidence' of crime. Warrants were permitted only to seize contraband, instrumentalities, or fruits of crime. In Hayden, the Court reversed course and held that the Fourth Amendment permitted the government to obtain search warrants to seize mere evidence. This ruling set the stage for a collision between law enforcement and the press. Because journalists and reporters often collect evidence of criminal activity in the course of developing news stories, they frequently possess 'mere evidence' of crime that may prove useful to law enforcement investigations. By freeing the Fourth Amendment from Boyd's restrictive regime, Hayden created the possibility that law enforcement could use search warrants to target the press for evidence of crime it had collected in the course of investigating and reporting news stories.

It did not take long for such a search to occur. On April 12, 1971, the District Attorney's Office in Santa Clara County, California obtained a search warrant to search the offices of The Stanford Daily, a Stanford University student newspaper. The DA's office was investigating a violent clash between the police and demonstrators that had occurred at the Stanford University Hospital three days earlier. The Stanford Daily had covered the incident, and published a special edition featuring photographs of the clash. Believing that the newspaper probably had more photographs of the clash that could help the police identify the demonstrators, the police obtained a warrant and sent four police officers to search the newspaper's office for further evidence that could assist the investigation. The officers found nothing. A month later, however, the Stanford Daily and its editors brought a civil suit against the police claiming that the search had violated their First and Fourth Amendment rights. The case ultimately reached the Supreme Court, and in Zurcher v. Stanford Daily, the Court rejected the newspaper's claims. Although the Court noted that 'the Fourth Amendment does not prevent or advise against legislative or executive efforts to establish nonconstitutional protections' for searches of the press, it held that neither the Fourth nor First Amendment prohibited such searches. Congress passed the PPA in 1980 in response to Stanford Daily. According to the Senate Report, the PPA protected 'the press and certain other persons not suspected of committing a crime with protections not provided currently by the Fourth Amendment.' The statute was intended to grant publishers certain statutory rights to discourage law enforcement officers from targeting publishers simply because they often gathered 'mere evidence' of crime.

As the legislative history indicates, the purpose of this statute is to limit searches for materials held by persons involved in First Amendment activities who are themselves not suspected of participation in the criminal activity for which the materials are sought, and not to limit the ability of law enforcement officers to search for and seize materials held by those suspected of committing the crime under investigation.

Subject to certain exceptions, the PPA makes it unlawful for a government officer 'to search for or seiz' materials when

(a) the materials are 'work product materials' prepared, produced, authored, or created 'in anticipation of communicating such materials to the public,'

(b) the materials include 'mental impressions, conclusions, or theories' of its creator, and

(c) the materials are possessed for the purpose of communicating the material to the public by a person 'reasonably believed to have a purpose to disseminate to the public' some form of 'public communication,'.

or

(a) the materials are 'documentary materials' that contain 'information,' and

(b) the materials are possessed by a person 'in connection with a purpose to disseminate to the public' some form of 'public communication.'

Although the language of the PPA is broad, the statute contains several exceptions. Searches will not violate the PPA when

1) the only materials searched for or seized are contraband, instrumentalities, or fruits of crime.

2) there is reason to believe that the immediate seizure of such materials is necessary to prevent death or serious bodily injury.

3) there is probable cause to believe that the person possessing such materials has committed or is committing the criminal offense to which the materials relate (an exception which is itself subject to several exceptions) and

4) in a search for or seizure of 'documentary materials' as defined by 2000aa-7(a), a subpoena has proven inadequate or there is reason to believe that a subpoena would not result in the production of the materials.

Violations of the PPA do not result in suppression of the evidence, but can result in civil damages against the sovereign whose officers or employees execute the search. If State officers or employees violate the PPA and the state does not waive its sovereign immunity and is thus immune from suit, individual State officers or employees may be held liable for acts within the scope or under the color of their employment subject to a reasonable good faith defense. PPA issues frequently arise in computer cases for two reasons that Congress could not have foreseen in 1980. First, the use of personal computers for publishing and the World Wide Web has dramatically expanded the scope of who is 'involved in First Amendment activities.' Today, anyone with a computer and access to the Internet may be a publisher who possesses PPA-protected materials on his or her computer.

The second reason that PPA issues arise frequently in computer cases is that the language of the statute does not explicitly rule out liability following incidental seizures of PPA-protected materials, and such seizures may inevitably result when agents search for and seize computer-stored contraband or evidence of crime that is commingled with PPA-protected materials. For example, investigations into illegal businesses that publish images of child pornography over the Internet have revealed that such businesses frequently support other publishing materials (such as drafts of adult pornography) that may be PPA-protected. Agents may find that the PPA interferes with their ability to seize the contraband child pornography because the contraband may be commingled with PPA-protected materials on the business's computers. Seizing the computer for the contraband would necessarily result in the seizure of the

PPA-protected materials. Under this interpretation of the PPA, the statute does not merely deter law enforcement from targeting innocent publishers for their evidence, but also affirmatively protects individuals from the incidental seizure of property that may be used in part for First Amendment activities.

As a formal matter, the legislative history and text of the PPA indicate that Congress probably intended the PPA to apply only when law enforcement intentionally targeted First Amendment material that related to a crime, as in Stanford Daily. For example, the so-called 'suspect exception' eliminates PPA liability when 'there is probable cause to believe that the person possessing such materials has committed or is committing the criminal offense to which the materials relate,'. This text indicates that Congress believed that PPA-protected materials would necessarily relate to a criminal offense, as when investigators target the materials as evidence.

When agents collaterally seize PPA-protected materials because they are commingled on a computer with other materials properly targeted by law enforcement, however, the PPA-protected materials will not necessarily relate to any crime at all. For example, the PPA-protected materials might be drafts of a horticulture newsletter that just happen to sit on the same hard drive as images of child pornography or records of a fraud scheme. At least one court has responded to this difficulty by reading the phrase 'to which the materials relate' quite broadly when an inadvertent seizure of commingled matter occurs. This reading effectively restores the suspect exception to its intended purpose: limiting the scope of PPA protection to 'the press and certain other persons not suspected of committing a crime.'

Although Congress probably intended the PPA to apply only when law enforcement intentionally targets PPA-protected materials in search of evidence, at least one court has held law enforcement liable under the PPA for the incidental seizure of (and more particularly, failure to return) PPA-protected materials stored on a seized computer. In Steve Jackson Games, Inc. v. Secret Service, aff'd on other grounds, a district court held the United States Secret Service liable for the inadvertent seizure of PPA-protected materials possessed by Steve Jackson Games, Inc. ('SJG'). Although SJG was primarily a publisher of role-playing games, it also operated a network of thirteen computers that provided its customers with e-mail, published information about SJG products, and stored drafts of upcoming publications. The Secret Service executed a search of SJG's computers on March 1, 1990, after learning that a system administrator of SJG's computers had been linked to a computer hacking incident under Secret Service investigation. Believing that the system administrator had stored evidence of the crime on SJG's computers, the Secret Service obtained a warrant and seized two of the thirteen computers connected to SJG's network, in addition to other materials.

The Secret Service did not know that SJG's computers contained publishing materials until the day after the search, on March 2, 1990. However, the Secret Service did not return the computers it seized until months later. At no time did the Secret Service believe that SJG itself was involved in the crime under investigation. The district court in Steve Jackson Games ruled that the Secret Service violated the PPA by continuing to hold SJG's seized property after it learned that the property included materials that SJG intended to disseminate to the public, including drafts of a book and magazine articles. Although the Secret Service had executed the search to find evidence of computer hacking, the incidental seizure and then retention of PPA-protected material constituted a prohibited seizure of 'work product materials' and 'documentary materials' according to 42 U.S.C. Unfortunately, the district court's precise reasoning in Steve Jackson Games is difficult to discern. For example, the court did not explain exactly which of the materials the Secret Service seized were covered by the PPA; instead, the court merely recited the property that had been seized, and concluded that some PPA-protected materials 'were obtained' during the search. Similarly, the court indicated that the search of SJG and the initial seizure of its property did not violate the PPA, but that the Secret Service's continued retention of SJG's property despite a request by SJG for its return was the true source of the PPA violation ' something that the statute itself does not appear to contemplate. The court also suggested that it might have ruled differently if the Secret Service had made 'copies of all information seized' and returned the hardware as soon as possible, but did not answer whether in fact it would have reached a different result in such case.

The court set damages equal to the company's lost profits resulting from the search, seizure, and retention of SJG's property, quite irrespective of how much of the company's lost profits were derived specifically from the seizure and retention of the PPA-protected materials. The boundaries of the PPA remain quite uncertain in the wake of Steve Jackson Games. See, e.g., State of Oklahoma v. One (1) Pioneer CD-ROM Changer, rejecting the apparent premise of Steve Jackson Games that the seizure of computer equipment could violate the

PPA merely because the equipment 'also contained or was used to disseminate potential 'documentary materials'). The handful of federal courts that have resolved civil suits filed under the PPA since the district court opinion in Steve Jackson Games have ruled against the plaintiffs with little substantive analysis. Agents and prosecutors who have reason to believe that a search may implicate the PPA should contact the Computer Crime and Intellectual Property Section or the Assistant U.S. Attorney designated as a Computer-Telecommunications Coordinator (CTC) in each district for more specific guidance.

When a search may result in the incidental seizure of network accounts belonging to innocent third parties, agents should take every step to protect the integrity of the third party accounts to avoid potential ECPA liability. When law enforcement executes a search of an Internet service provider and seizes the accounts of customers and subscribers, those customers and subscribers may bring civil actions claiming that the search violated the Electronic Communications Privacy Act (ECPA). ECPA governs law enforcement access to the contents of electronic communications stored by third-party service providers. In addition, ECPA has a criminal provision that prohibits unauthorized access to electronic or wire communications in 'electronic storage.' The concern that a search executed pursuant to a valid warrant might violate ECPA derives from Steve Jackson Games, Inc. v. Secret Service. In Steve Jackson Games, the district court held the Secret Service liable under ECPA after it seized, reviewed, and (in some cases) deleted stored electronic communications seized pursuant to a valid search warrant. The court's holding appears to be rooted in the mistaken belief that ECPA requires that search warrants also comply with and the various notice requirements of ' In fact, ECPA makes quite clear that ' and the notice requirements ' 2703 are implicated only when law enforcement does not obtain a search warrant. Indeed, the text of ECPA does not appear to contemplate civil liability for searches and seizures authorized by valid Rule 41 search warrants: ECPA expressly authorizes government access to stored communications pursuant to a warrant issued under the Federal Rules of Criminal Procedure, and the criminal prohibition does not apply when access is authorized under ' 2703. Further, objectively reasonable good faith reliance on a warrant, court order, or statutory authorization is a complete defense to an ECPA violation.

The best way to square the result in Steve Jackson Games with the plain language of ECPA is to exercise great caution when agents need to execute searches of Internet service providers and other third-parties holding stored wire or electronic communications. In most cases, investigators will want to avoid a wholesale search and seizure of the provider's computers. When investigators have no choice but to execute the search, they must take special care. For example, if agents have reason to believe that they may seize customer accounts belonging to innocent persons but have no reason to believe that the evidence sought will be stored there, they should inform the magistrate judge in the search warrant affidavit that they will not search those accounts and should take steps to ensure the confidentiality of the accounts in light of the privacy concerns expressed. Safeguarding the accounts of innocent persons absent specific reasons to believe that evidence may be stored in the persons' accounts should satisfy the concerns expressed in Steve Jackson Games. If agents believe that a hacker or system administrator might have hidden evidence of a crime in the account of an innocent customer or subscriber, agents should proceed carefully. For example, agents should inform the magistrate judge of their need to search the account in the affidavit, and should attempt to obtain the consent of the customer or subscriber if feasible. In such cases, agents should contact the Computer Crime and Intellectual Property Section or the CTC designated in their district for more specific guidance.

A search is constitutional if it does not violate a person's 'reasonable' or 'legitimate' expectation of privacy. This inquiry embraces two discrete questions: first, whether the individual's conduct reflects 'an actual (subjective) expectation of privacy,' and second, whether the individual's subjective expectation of privacy is 'one that society is prepared to recognize as "reasonable." In most cases, the difficulty of contesting a defendant's subjective expectation of privacy focuses the analysis on the objective aspect of the Katz test, i.e., whether the individual's expectation of privacy was reasonable. No bright line rule indicates whether an expectation of privacy is constitutionally reasonable. For example, the Supreme Court has held that a person has a reasonable expectation of privacy in property located inside a person's home, in conversations taking place in an enclosed phone booth, and in the contents of opaque containers. In contrast, a person does not have a reasonable expectation of privacy in activities conducted in open fields, in garbage deposited at the outskirts of real property, or in a stranger's house that the person has entered without the owner's consent in order to commit a theft.

To determine whether an individual has a reasonable expectation of privacy in information stored in a computer, it helps to treat the computer like a closed container such as a briefcase or file cabinet. The Fourth Amendment generally prohibits law enforcement from accessing and viewing information stored in a computer without a warrant if it would be prohibited from opening a closed container and examining its contents in the same situation. The most basic Fourth Amendment question in computer cases asks whether an individual enjoys a reasonable expectation of privacy in electronic information stored within computers (or other electronic storage devices) under the individual's control. For example, do individuals have a reasonable expectation of privacy in the contents of their laptop computers, floppy disks or pagers? If the answer is 'yes,' then the government ordinarily must obtain a warrant before it accesses the information stored inside.

When confronted with this issue, courts have analogized electronic storage devices to closed containers, and have reasoned that accessing the information stored within an electronic storage device is akin to opening a closed container. Because individuals generally retain a reasonable expectation of privacy in the contents of closed containers, they also generally retain a reasonable expectation of privacy in data held within electronic storage devices. Accordingly, accessing information stored in a computer ordinarily will implicate the owner's reasonable expectation of privacy in the information. Although individuals generally retain a reasonable expectation of privacy in computers under their control, special circumstances may eliminate that expectation. For example, an individual will not retain a reasonable expectation of privacy in information from a computer that the person has made openly available. Agents looking over the defendant's shoulder read the defendant's password from the screen as the defendant typed his password into a handheld computer. The court found no Fourth Amendment violation in obtaining the password, because the defendant did not enjoy a reasonable expectation of privacy 'in the display that appeared on the screen.' Nor will individuals generally enjoy a reasonable expectation of privacy in the contents of computers they have stolen.

Individuals who retain a reasonable expectation of privacy in stored electronic information under their control may lose Fourth Amendment protections when they relinquish that control to third parties. For example, an individual may offer a container of electronic information to a third party by bringing a malfunctioning computer to a repair shop, or by shipping a floppy diskette in the mail to a friend. Alternatively, a user may transmit information to third parties electronically, such as by sending data across the Internet. When law enforcement agents learn of information possessed by third parties that may provide evidence of a crime, they may wish to inspect it. Whether the Fourth Amendment requires them to obtain a warrant before examining the information depends first upon whether the third-party possession has eliminated the individual's reasonable expectation of privacy.

To analyze third-party possession issues, it helps first to distinguish between possession by a carrier in the course of transmission to an intended recipient, and subsequent possession by the intended recipient. For example, if A hires B to carry a package to C, A's reasonable expectation of privacy in the contents of the package during the time that B carries the package on its way to C may be different than A's reasonable expectation of privacy after C has received the package. During transmission, contents generally retain Fourth Amendment protection.

The government ordinarily may not examine the contents of a package in the course of transmission without a warrant. Government intrusion and examination of the contents ordinarily violates the reasonable expectation of privacy of both the sender and receiver. This rule applies regardless of whether the carrier is owned by the government or a private company.

A government 'search' of an intangible electronic signal in the course of transmission may also implicate the Fourth Amendment. Its scope encompasses, and in many significant ways exceeds, the protection offered by the Fourth Amendment. As a practical matter, then, the monitoring of wire and electronic communications in the course of transmission generally raises many statutory questions, but few constitutional ones.

Once an item has been received by the intended recipient, the sender's reasonable expectation of privacy generally depends upon whether the sender can reasonably expect to retain control over the item and its contents. When a person leaves a package with a third party for temporary safekeeping, for example, he usually retains control of the package, and thus retains a reasonable expectation of privacy in its contents. If the sender cannot reasonably expect to retain control over the item in the third party's possession, however, the sender no longer retains a reasonable expectation of privacy in its contents. The defendant e-mailed confidential pricing information relating to his employer to his employer's competitor. After the FBI searched the competitor's computers and found the pricing information, the defendant claimed that the search violated his Fourth Amendment rights.

The Fourth Circuit disagreed, holding that the defendant relinquished his interest in and control over the information by sending it to the competitor for the competitor's future use. In some cases, the sender may initially retain a right to control the third party's possession, but may lose that right over time. The general rule is that the sender's Fourth Amendment rights dissipate along with the sender's right to control the third party's possession. For example, in United States v. Poulsen, computer hacker Kevin Poulsen left computer tapes in a locker at a commercial storage facility but neglected to pay rent for the locker. Following a warrantless search of the facility, the government sought to use the tapes against Poulsen. The Ninth Circuit held that the search did not violate Poulsen's reasonable expectation of privacy because under state law Poulsen's failure to pay rent extinguished his right to access the tapes.

An important line of Supreme Court cases states that individuals generally cannot reasonably expect to retain control over mere information revealed to third parties, even if the senders have a subjective expectation that the third parties will keep the information confidential. For example, in United States v. Miller, the Court held that the Fourth Amendment does not protect bank account information that account holders divulge to their banks. By placing information under the control of a third party, the Court stated, an account holder assumes the risk that the information will be conveyed to the government. Id. According to the Court, 'the Fourth Amendment does not prohibit the obtaining of information revealed to a third party and conveyed by him to Government authorities, even if the information is revealed on the assumption that it will be used only for a limited purpose and the confidence placed in the third party will not be betrayed.' Because computer data is 'information,' this line of cases suggests that individuals who send data over communications networks may lose Fourth Amendment protection in the data once it reaches the intended recipient. Of course, the absence of constitutional protections does not necessarily mean that the government can access the data without a warrant or court order. Statutory protections exist that generally protect the privacy of electronic communications stored remotely with service providers, and can protect the privacy of Internet users when the Fourth Amendment may not.

Defendants will occasionally raise a Fourth Amendment challenge to the acquisition of account records and subscriber information held by Internet service providers using less process than a full search warrant. As discussed in a later chapter, the Electronic Communications Privacy Act permits the government to obtain transactional records with an 'articulable facts' court order, and basic subscriber information with a subpoena. These statutory procedures comply with the Fourth Amendment because customers of Internet service providers do not have a reasonable expectation of privacy in customer account records maintained by and for the provider's business. This rule accords with prior cases considering the scope of Fourth Amendment protection in customer account records.

The Fourth Amendment 'is wholly inapplicable to a search or seizure, even an unreasonable one, effected by a private individual not acting as an agent of the Government or with the participation or knowledge of any governmental official.' As a result, no violation of the Fourth Amendment occurs when a private individual acting on his own accord conducts a search and makes the results available to law enforcement. For example, in United States v. Hall, the defendant took his computer to a private computer specialist for repairs. In the course of evaluating the defendant's computer, the repairman observed that many files stored on the computer had filenames characteristic of child pornography. The repairman accessed the files, saw that they did in fact contain child pornography, and then contacted the state police. The tip led to a warrant, the defendant's arrest, and his conviction for child pornography offenses. On appeal, the Seventh Circuit rejected the defendant's claim that the repairman's warrantless search through the computer violated the Fourth Amendment. Because the repairman's search was conducted on his own, the court held, the Fourth Amendment did not apply to the search or his later description of the evidence to the state police.

In United States v. Jacobsen, the Supreme Court presented the framework that should guide agents seeking to uncover evidence as a result of a private search. According to Jacobsen, agents who learn of evidence via a private search can reenact the original private search without violating any reasonable expectation of privacy. What the agents cannot do without a warrant is 'exceed[] the scope of the private search.' This standard requires agents to limit their investigation to the precise scope of the private search when searching without a warrant after a private search has occurred. So long as the agents limit themselves to the scope of the private search, the agents' search will not violate the Fourth Amendment. However, as soon as agents exceed the scope of the private warrantless search, any evidence uncovered may be suppressed. In computer cases, this aspect of Jacobsen means that private searches will often be useful partly as opportunities to provide the probable cause needed to obtain a warrant for a further search. The fact that a private person has uncovered evidence of a crime on another person's computer does not permit agents to search the entire computer. Instead, the private search permits the agents to view the evidence that the private search revealed, and, if necessary, to use that evidence as a basis for procuring a warrant to search the rest of the computer.

Although most private search issues arise when private third parties intentionally examine property and offer evidence of a crime to law enforcement, the same framework applies when third parties inadvertently expose evidence of a crime to plain view. For example, in United States v. Procopio, a defendant stored incriminating files in his brother's safe. Later, thieves stole the safe, opened it, and abandoned it in a public park. Police investigating the theft of the safe found the files scattered on the ground nearby, gathered them, and then used them against the defendant in an unrelated case. The First Circuit held that the use of the files did not violate the Fourth Amendment, because the files were made openly available by the thieves' private search.

The person conducting a search is not a government employee does not necessarily mean that the search is 'private' for Fourth Amendment purposes. A search by a private party will be considered a Fourth Amendment government search 'if the private party act[s] as an instrument or agent of the Government.' Skinner v.

Railway Labor Executives' Ass'n,. The Supreme Court has offered little guidance on when private conduct can be attributed to the government; the Court has merely stated that this question 'necessarily turns on the degree of the Government's participation in the private party's activities, . . . a question that can only be resolved "in light of all the circumstances". In the absence of a more definitive standard, the various federal Courts of Appeals have adopted a range of approaches for distinguishing between private and government searches. About half of the circuits apply a 'totality of the circumstances' approach that examines three factors: whether the government knows of or acquiesces in the intrusive conduct; whether the party performing the search intends to assist law enforcement efforts at the time of the search; and whether the government affirmatively encourages, initiates or instigates the private action. Other circuits have adopted more rule-like formulations that focus on only two of these factors.

Warrantless searches that violate a reasonable expectation of privacy will comply with the Fourth Amendment if they fall within an established exception to the warrant requirement. Cases involving computers often raise questions relating to how these 'established' exceptions apply to new technologies. Agents may search a place or object without a warrant or even probable cause if a person with authority has voluntarily consented to the search. This consent may be explicit or implicit. Whether consent was voluntarily given is a question of fact that the court must decide by considering the totality of the circumstances. While no single aspect controls the result, the Supreme Court has identified the following important factors: the age, education, intelligence, physical and mental condition of the person giving consent; whether the person was under arrest; and whether the person had been advised of his right to refuse consent. The government carries the burden of proving that consent was voluntary. In computer crime cases, two consent issues arise particularly often. First, when does a search exceed the scope of consent? For example, when a target consents to the search of a machine, to what extent does the consent authorize the retrieval of information stored in the machine? Second, who is the proper party to consent to a search? Do roommates, friends, and parents have the authority to consent to a search of another person's computer files?

'The scope of a consent to search is generally defined by its expressed object, and is limited by the breadth of the consent given.' The standard for measuring the scope of consent under the Fourth Amendment is objective reasonableness: 'What would the typical reasonable person have understood by the exchange between the [agent] and the [person granting consent]' This requires a fact-intensive inquiry into whether it was reasonable for the agent to believe that the scope of consent included the items searched. Id. Of course, when the limits of the consent are clearly given, either before or during the search, agents must respect these bounds.

Computer cases often raise the question of whether consent to search a location or item implicitly includes consent to access the memory of electronic storage devices encountered during the search. In such cases, courts look to whether the particular circumstances of the agents' request for consent implicitly or explicitly limited the scope of the search to a particular type, scope, or duration. Because this approach ultimately relies on fact-driven notions of common sense, results reached in published opinions have hinged upon subtle (if not entirely inscrutable) distinctions. Prosecutors can strengthen their argument that the scope of consent included consent to search electronic storage devices by relying on analogous cases involving closed containers. Agents should be especially careful about relying on consent as the basis for a search of a computer when they obtain consent for one reason but then wish to conduct a search for another reason. In two recent cases, the Courts of Appeals suppressed images of child pornography found on computers after agents procured the defendant's consent to search his property for other evidence.

In United States v. Turner, detectives searching for physical evidence of an attempted sexual assault obtained written consent from the victim's neighbor to search the neighbor's 'premises' and 'personal property.' Before the neighbor signed the consent form, the detectives discovered a large knife and blood stains in his apartment, and explained to him that they were looking for more evidence of the assault that the suspect might have left behind. While several agents searched for physical evidence, one detective searched the contents of the neighbor's personal computer and discovered stored images of child pornography. The neighbor was charged with possessing child pornography. On interlocutory appeal, the First Circuit held that the search of the computer exceeded the scope of consent and suppressed the evidence. According to the Court, the detectives' statements that they were looking for signs of the assault limited the scope of consent to the kind of physical evidence that an intruder might have left behind. By transforming the search for physical evidence into a search for computer files, the detective had exceeded the scope of consent. Because the decisions evaluating the scope of consent to search computers have reached sometimes unpredictable results, investigators should indicate the scope of the search explicitly when obtaining a suspect's consent to search a computer.

It is common for several people to use or own the same computer equipment. If any one of those people gives permission to search for data, agents may generally rely on that consent, so long as the person has authority over the computer. In such cases, all users have assumed the risk that a co-user might discover everything in the computer, and might also permit law enforcement to search this 'common area' as well. The watershed case in this area is United States v. Matlock. In Matlock, the Supreme Court stated that one who has 'common authority' over premises or effects may consent to a search even if an absent co-user objects. According to the Court, the common authority that establishes the right of third-party consent requires mutual use of the property by persons generally having joint access or control for most purposes, so that it is reasonable to recognize that any of the co-inhabitants has the right to permit the inspection in his own right and that the others have assumed the risk that one of their number might permit the common area to be searched. Under the Matlock approach, a private third party may consent to a search of property under the third party's joint access or control. Agents may view what the third party may see without violating any reasonable expectation of privacy so long as they limit the search to the zone of the consenting third party's common authority. This rule often requires agents to inquire into third parties's rights of access before conducting a consent search, and to draw lines between those areas that fall within the third party's common authority and those areas outside of the third party's control. Because the joint access test does not require a unity of interests between the suspect and the third party, however, Matlock permits third-party consent even when the target of the search is present and refuses to consent to the search.

Courts have not squarely addressed whether a suspect's decision to password-protect or encrypt files stored in a jointly-used computer denies co-users the right to consent to a search of the files under Matlock. However, it appears likely that encryption and password-protection would in most cases indicate the absence of common authority to consent to a search among co-users who do not know the password or possess the encryption key. Conversely, if the co-user has been given the password or encryption key by the suspect, then she probably has the requisite common authority to consent to a search of the files under Matlock. As a practical matter, agents may have little way of knowing the precise bounds of a third party's common authority when the agents obtain third-party consent to conduct a search. When queried, consenting third parties may falsely claim that they have common authority over property.

In Illinois v. Rodriguez, the Supreme Court held that the Fourth Amendment does not automatically require suppression of evidence discovered during a consent search when it later comes to light that the third party who consented to the search lacked the authority to do so. Instead, the Court held that agents can rely on a claim of authority to consent if based on 'the facts available to the officer at the moment, . . . a man of reasonable caution . . . [would believe] that the consenting party had authority' to consent to a search of the premises. When agents reasonably rely on apparent authority to consent, the resulting search does not violate the Fourth Amendment.

Absent an affirmative showing that the consenting spouse has no access to the property searched, the courts generally hold that either spouse may consent to search all of the couple's property. For example, in United States v. Smith, a man named Smith was living with a woman named Ushman and her two daughters. When allegations of child molestation were raised against Smith, Ushman consented to the search of his computer, which was located in the house in an alcove connected to the master bedroom. Although Ushman used Smith's computer only rarely, the district court held that she could consent to the search of Smith's computer. Because Ushman was not prohibited from entering the alcove and Smith had not password-protected the computer, the court reasoned, she had authority to consent to the search. Even if she lacked actual authority to consent, the court added, she had apparent authority to consent.

In some computer crime cases, the perpetrators are relatively young and reside with their parents. When the perpetrator is a minor, parental consent to search the perpetrator's property and living space will almost always be valid. When the sons and daughters who reside with their parents are legal adults, however, the issue is more complicated. Under Matlock, it is clear that parents may consent to a search of common areas in the family home regardless of the perpetrator's age. When agents would like to search an adult child's room or other private areas, however, agents cannot assume that the adult's parents have authority to consent. Although courts have offered divergent approaches, they have paid particular attention to three factors: the suspect's age;

whether the suspect pays rent; and whether the suspect has taken affirmative steps to deny his or her parents access to the suspect's room or private area. When suspects are older, pay rent, and/or deny access to parents, courts have generally held that parents may not consent. In contrast, parents usually may consent if their adult children do not pay rent, are fairly young, and have taken no steps to deny their parents access to the space to be searched.

Every computer network is managed by a 'system administrator' or 'system operator' whose job is to keep the network running smoothly, monitor security, and repair the network when problems arise. System operators have 'root level' access to the systems they administer, which effectively grants them master keys to open any account and read any file on their systems. When investigators suspect that a network account contains relevant evidence, they may feel inclined to seek the system administrator's consent to search the contents of that account. As a practical matter, the primary barrier to searching a network account pursuant to a system administrator's consent is statutory, not constitutional. System administrators typically serve as agents of 'provider[s] of electronic communication service' under the Electronic Communications Privacy Act ('ECPA'). ECPA regulates law enforcement efforts to obtain the consent of a system administrator to search an individual's account. Accordingly, any attempt to obtain a system administrator's consent to search an account must comply with ECPA. 'The Electronic Communications Privacy Act.' To the extent that ECPA authorizes system administrators to consent to searches, the resulting consent searches will in most cases comply with the Fourth Amendment. The first reason is that individuals may not retain a reasonable expectation of privacy in the remotely stored files and records that their network accounts contain. If an individual does not retain a constitutionally reasonable expectation of privacy in his remotely stored files, it will not matter whether the system administrator has the necessary joint control over the account needed to satisfy the Matlock test because a subsequent search will not violate the Fourth Amendment.

In the event that a court holds that an individual does possess a reasonable expectation of privacy in remotely stored account files, whether a system administrator's consent would satisfy Matlock should depend on the circumstances. Clearly, the system administrator's access to all network files does not by itself provide the common authority that triggers authority to consent. In the pre-Matlock case of Stoner v. California, the Supreme Court held that a hotel clerk lacked the authority to consent to the search of a hotel room. Although the clerk was permitted to enter the room to perform his duties, and the guest had left his room key with the clerk, the Court concluded that the clerk could not consent to the search. If the hotel guest's protection from unreasonable searches and seizures 'were left to depend on the unfettered discretion of an employee of the hotel,' Justice Stewart reasoned, it would 'disappear.' To the extent that the access of a system operator to a network account is analogous to the access of a hotel clerk to a hotel room, the claim that a system operator may consent to a search of Fourth Amendment-protected files is weak. Of course, the hotel clerk analogy may be inadequate in some circumstances. For example, an employee generally does not have the same relationship with the system administrator of his company's network as a customer of a private ISP such as AOL might have with the ISP's system administrator. The company may grant the system administrator of the company network full rights to access employee accounts for any work-related reason, and the employees may know that the system administrator has such access. In circumstances such as this, the system administrator would likely have sufficient common authority over the accounts to be able to consent to a search. Further, in the case of a government network, the Fourth Amendment rules would likely differ dramatically from the rules that apply to private networks.

Individuals often enter into agreements with the government in which they waive some of their Fourth Amendment rights. For example, prison guards may agree to be searched for drugs as a condition of employment, and visitors to government buildings may agree to a limited search of their person and property as a condition of entrance. Similarly, users of computer systems may waive their rights to privacy as a condition of using the systems. When individuals who have waived their rights are then searched and challenge the searches on Fourth Amendment grounds, courts typically focus on whether the waiver eliminated the individual's reasonable expectation of privacy against the search. A few courts have approached the same problem from a slightly different direction and have asked whether the waiver established implied consent to the search. According to the doctrine of implied consent, consent to a search may be inferred from an individual's conduct. For example, in United States v. Ellis, a civilian visiting a naval air station agreed to post a visitor's pass on the windshield of his car as a condition of bringing the car on the base. The pass stated that '[a]cceptance of this pass gives your consent to search this vehicle while entering, aboard, or leaving this station.' During the visitor's stay on the base, a station investigator who suspected that the visitor had stored marijuana in the car approached the visitor and asked him if he had read the pass. After the visitor admitted that he had, the investigator searched the car and found 20 plastic bags containing marijuana. The Fifth Circuit ruled that the warrantless search of the car was permissible, because the visitor had impliedly consented to the search when he knowingly and voluntarily entered the base with full knowledge of the terms of the visitor's pass. Ellis notwithstanding, it must be noted that several circuits have been critical of the implied consent doctrine in the Fourth Amendment context. Despite the Fifth Circuit's broad construction, other courts have proven reluctant to apply the doctrine absent evidence that the suspect actually knew of the search and voluntarily consented to it at the time the search occurred. Absent such evidence, these courts have preferred to examine general waivers of Fourth Amendment rights solely under the reasonable-expectation-of-privacy test.

Under the 'exigent circumstances' exception to the warrant requirement, agents can search without a warrant if the circumstances 'would cause a reasonable person to believe that entry . . . was necessary to prevent physical harm to the officers or other persons, the destruction of relevant evidence, the escape of the suspect, or some other consequence improperly frustrating legitimate law enforcement efforts. In determining whether exigent circumstances exist, agents should consider: (1) the degree of urgency involved, (2) the amount of time necessary to obtain a warrant, (3) whether the evidence is about to be removed or destroyed, (4) the possibility of danger at the site, (5) information indicating the possessors of the contraband know the police are on their trail, and (6) the ready destructibility of the contraband. Exigent circumstances often arise in computer cases because electronic data is perishable. Computer commands can destroy data in a matter of seconds, as can humidity, temperature, physical mutilation, or magnetic fields created, for example, by passing a strong magnet over a disk. For example, in United States v. David, agents saw the defendant deleting files on his computer memo book, and seized the computer immediately. The district court held that the agents did not need a warrant to seize the memo book because the defendant's acts had created exigent circumstances. Similarly, in United States v. Romero-Garcia, aff'd on other grounds, a district court held that agents had properly accessed the information in an electronic pager in their possession because they had reasonably believed that it was necessary to prevent the destruction of evidence.

The information stored in pagers is readily destroyed, the court noted: incoming messages can delete stored information, and batteries can die, erasing the information. Accordingly, the agents were justified in accessing the pager without first acquiring a warrant. Of course, in computer cases, as in all others, the existence of exigent circumstances is absolutely tied to the facts. Importantly, the existence of exigent circumstances does not permit agents to search or seize beyond what is necessary to prevent the destruction of the evidence. When the exigency ends, the right to conduct warrantless searches does as well: the need to take certain steps to prevent the destruction of evidence does not authorize agents to take further steps without a warrant.

Accordingly, the seizure of computer hardware to prevent the dest ruction of information it contains will not ordinarily support a subsequent search of that information without a warrant.

Evidence of a crime may be seized without a warrant under the plain view exception to the warrant requirement. To rely on this exception, the agent must be in a lawful position to observe and access the evidence, and its incriminating character must be immediately apparent. For example, if an agent conducts a valid search of a hard drive and comes across evidence of an unrelated crime while conducting the search, the agent may seize the evidence under the plain view doctrine. Importantly, the plain view exception cannot justify violations of an individual's reasonable expectation of privacy. The exception merely permits the seizure of evidence that has already been viewed in accordance with the Fourth Amendment. In computer cases, this means that the government cannot rely on the plain view exception to justify opening a closed computer file. The contents of a file that must be opened to be viewed are not in 'plain view.' This rule accords with decisions applying the plain view exception to closed containers.

United States v. Carey, provides a useful example. In Carey, a police detective searching a hard drive with a warrant for drug trafficking evidence opened a 'jpg' file and instead discovered child pornography. At that point, the detective abandoned the search for drug trafficking evidence and spent five hours accessing and downloading several hundred 'jpg' files in a search for more child pornography. When the defendant moved to exclude the child pornography files on the ground that they were seized beyond the scope of the warrant, the government argued that the detective had seized the 'jpg' files properly because the contents of the contraband files were in plain view. The Tenth Circuit rejected this argument with respect to all of the files except for the first 'jpg' file the detective discovered. Although the court's reasoning is somewhat opaque, this aspect of Carey seems sensible. The plain view exception permits agents to seize property found in plain view, not to infringe a suspect's right to privacy until his property comes into plain view. As a result, the detective could seize the first 'jpg' file that came into plain view when the detective was executing the search warrant, but could not rely on the plain view exception to justify the search for additional 'jpg' files on the defendant's computers that were beyond the scope of the warrant.

Pursuant to a lawful arrest, agents may conduct a 'full search' of the arrested person, and a more limited search of his surrounding area, without a warrant. For example, in Robinson, a police officer conducting a patdown search incident to an arrest for a traffic offense discovered a crumpled cigarette package in the suspect's left breast pocket. Not knowing what the package contained, the officer opened the package and discovered fourteen capsules of heroin. The Supreme Court held that the search of the package was permissible, even though the officer had no articulable reason to open the package. In light of the general need to preserve evidence and prevent harm to the arresting officer, the Court reasoned, it was perse reasonable for an officer to conduct a 'full search of the person' pursuant to a lawful arrest. Due to the increasing use of handheld and portable computers and other electronic storage devices, agents often encounter computers when conducting searches incident to lawful arrests. Suspects may be carrying pagers,

Personal Digital Assistants (such as Palm Pilots), or even laptop computers when they are arrested. Does the search-incident-to-arrest exception permit an agent to access the memory of an electronic storage device found on the arrestee's person during a warrantless search incident to arrest? In the case of electronic pagers, the answer clearly is 'yes.' Relying on Robinson, courts have uniformly permitted agents to access electronic pagers carried by the arrested person at the time of arrest.

Courts have not yet addressed whether Robinson will permit warrantless searches of electronic storage devices that contain more information than pagers. In the paper world, certainly, cases have allowed extensive searches of written materials discovered incident to lawful arrests. For example, courts have uniformly held that agents may inspect the entire contents of a suspect's wallet found on his person. Similarly, one court has held that agents could photocopy the entire contents of an address book found on the defendant's person during the arrest, and others have permitted the search of a defendant's briefcase that was at his side at the time of arrest. If agents can examine the contents of wallets, address books, and briefcases without a warrant, it could be argued that they should be able to search their electronic counterparts (such as electronic organizers, floppy disks, and Palm Pilots) as well.The limit on this argument is that any search incident to an arrest must be reasonable. While a search of physical items found on the arrestee's person may always be reasonable, more invasive searches in different circumstances may violate the Fourth Amendment. For example, the increasing storage capacity of handheld computers suggests that Robinson's bright line rule may not always apply in the case of electronic searches.

Courts may conclude that a quick search through a pager that stores a few phone numbers is reasonable incident to an arrest, but that a very time-consuming search through a handheld computer that contains an entire warehouse of information presents a different case. When in doubt, agents should obtain a search warrant before examining the contents of electronic storage devices that might contain large amounts of information.

Law enforcement officers routinely inventory the items they have seized. Such 'inventory searches' are reasonable — and therefore fall under an exception to the warrant requirement — when two conditions are met. First, the search must serve a legitimate, non-investigatory purpose that outweighs the intrusion on the individual's Fourth Amendment rights. Second, the search must follow standardized procedures. It is unlikely that the inventory-search exception to the warrant requirement would support a search through seized computer files.

Even assuming that standard procedures authorized such a search, the legitimate purposes served by inventory searches in the physical world do not translate well into the intangible realm. Information does not generally need to be reviewed to be protected, and does not pose a risk of physical danger. Although an owner could claim that his computer files were altered or deleted while in police custody, examining the contents of the files would offer little protection from tampering. Accordingly, agents will generally need to obtain a search warrant in order to examine seized computer files held in custody.

In order to protect the government's ability to monitor contraband and other property that may enter or exit the United States illegally, the Supreme Court has recognized a special exception to the warrant requirement for searches that occur at the border of the United States. According to the Court, 'routine searches' at the border or its functional equivalent do not require a warrant, probable cause, or even reasonable suspicion that the search may uncover contraband or evidence. Searches that are especially intrusive require at least reasonable suspicion, however. These rules apply to people and property both entering and exiting the United States. At least one court has interpreted the border search exception to permit a warrantless search of a computer disk for contraband computer files. In United States v. Roberts, United States Customs Agents learned that William Roberts, a suspect believed to be carrying computerized images of child pornography, was scheduled to fly from Houston, Texas to Paris, France on a particular day.

On the day of the flight, the agents set up an inspection area in the jetway at the Houston airport with the sole purpose of searching Roberts. Roberts arrived at the inspection area and was told by the agents that they were searching for 'currency' and 'high technology or other data' that could not be exported legally. After the agents searched Roberts' property and found a laptop computer and six Zip diskettes, Roberts agreed to sign a consent form permitting the agents to search his property. A subsequent search revealed several thousand images of child pornography. When charges were brought, Roberts moved for suppression of the computer files, but the district court ruled that the search had not violated the Fourth Amendment. According to the court, the search of Roberts' luggage had been a 'routine search' for which no suspicion was required, even though the justification for the search offered by the agents merely had been a pretext. The court also concluded that Roberts' consent justified the search of the laptop and diskettes, and indicated that even if Roberts had not consented to the search, '[t]he search of the defendant's computer and diskettes would have been a routine export search, valid under the Fourth Amendment.'

Importantly, agents and prosecutors should not interpret Roberts as permitting the interception of data transmitted electronically to and from the United States. Any real-time interception of electronically transmitted data in the United States must comply strictly with the requirements. Further, once electronically transferred data from outside the United States arrives at its destination within the United States, the government ordinarily cannot rely on the border search exception to search for and seize the data because the data is no longer at the border or its functional equivalent.

Warrantless workplace searches deserve a separate analysis because they occur often in computer cases and raise unusually complicated legal issues. The primary cause of the analytical difficulty is the Supreme Court's complex decision in O'Connor v. Ortega. Under O'Connor, the legality of warrantless workplace searches depends on often-subtle factual distinctions such as whether the workplace is public sector or private sector, whether employment policies exist that authorize a search, and whether the search is work-related.

Every warrantless workplace search must be evaluated carefully on its facts. In general, however, law enforcement officers can conduct a warrantless search of private (i.e., non-government) workplaces only if the officers obtain the consent of either the employer or another employee with common authority over the area searched. In public (i.e., government) workplaces, officers cannot rely on an employer's consent, but can conduct searches if written employment policies or office practices establish that the government employees targeted by the search cannot reasonably expect privacy in their workspace. Further, government employers and supervisors can conduct reasonable work-related searches of employee workspaces without a warrant even if the searches violate employees' reasonable expectation of privacy. One cautionary note is in order before we proceed. This discussion evaluates the legality of warrantless workplace searches of computers under the Fourth Amendment. In many cases, however, workplace searches will implicate federal privacy statutes in addition to the Fourth Amendment. For example, efforts to obtain an employee's files and e-mail from the employer's network server raise issues under the Electronic Communications Privacy Act, 18 U.S.C. and workplace monitoring of an employee's Before conducting a workplace search, investigators must make sure that their search will not violate either the Fourth Amendment or relevant federal privacy statutes.

The rules for conducting warrantless searches and seizures in private-sector workplaces generally mirror the rules for conducting warrantless searches in homes and other personal residences. Private company employees generally retain a reasonable expectation of privacy in their workplaces. As a result, private-workplace searches by law enforcement will usually require a warrant unless the agents can obtain the consent of an employer or a co-worker with common authority. Private-sector employees will usually retain a reasonable expectation of privacy in their office space. In Mancusi v. DeForte, police officers conducted a warrantless search of an office at a local union headquarters that defendant Frank DeForte shared with several other union officials. In response to DeForte's claim that the search violated his Fourth Amendment rights, the police officers argued that the joint use of the space by DeForte's co-workers made his expectation of privacy unreasonable. The Court disagreed, stating that DeForte 'still could reasonably have expected that only [his officemates] and their personal or business guests would enter the office, and that records would not be touched except with their permission or that of union higher-ups.' Because only a specific group of people actually enjoyed joint access and use of DeForte's office, the officers' presence violated DeForte's reasonable expectation of privacy. As a practical matter, then, private employees will generally retain an expectation of privacy in their work space unless that space is 'open to the world at large.'

Although most non-government workplaces will support a reasonable expectation of privacy from a law enforcement search, agents can defeat this expectation by obtaining the consent of a party who exercises common authority over the area searched. In practice, this means that agents can often overcome the warrant requirement by obtaining the consent of the target's employer or supervisor. Depending on the facts, a co-worker's consent may suffice as well. Private-sector employers and supervisors generally enjoy a broad authority to consent to searches in the workplace. For example, in United States v. Gargiso, a pre-Matlock case, agents conducting a criminal investigation of an employee of a private company sought access to a locked, wired-off area in the employer's basement.

The agents explained their needs to the company's vice-president, who took the agents to the basement and opened the basement with his key. When the employee attempted to suppress the evidence that the agents discovered in the basement, the court held that the vice-president's consent was effective. Because the vice-president shared supervisory power over the basement with the employee, the court reasoned, he could consent to the agents' search of that area. In a close case, an employment policy or computer network banner that establishes the employer's right to consent to a workplace search can help establish the employer's common authority to consent under Matlock.

Agents should be careful about relying on a co-worker's consent to conduct a workplace search. While employers generally retain the right to access their employees' work spaces, co-workers may or may not, depending on the facts. When co-workers do exercise common authority over a workspace, however, investigators can rely on a co-worker's consent to search that space. For example, in United States v. Buettner-Janusch, a professor and an undergraduate research assistant at New York University consented to a search of an NYU laboratory managed by a second professor suspected of using his laboratory to manufacture LSD and other drugs. Although the search involved opening vials and several other closed containers, the Second Circuit held that Matlock authorized the search because both consenting co-workers had been authorized to make full use of the lab for their research.

Warrantless workplace searches by private employers rarely violate the Fourth Amendment. So long as the employer is not acting as an instrument or agent of the Government at the time of the search, the search is a private search and the Fourth Amendment does not apply. Although warrantless computer searches in private-sector workplaces follow familiar Fourth Amendment rules, the application of the Fourth Amendment to public-sector workplace searches of computers presents a different matter. In O'Connor v. Ortega, the Supreme Court introduced a distinct framework for evaluating warrantless searches in government workplaces that applies to computer searches. According to O'Connor, a government employee can enjoy a reasonable expectation of privacy in his workplace. However, an expectation of privacy becomes unreasonable if 'actual office practices and procedures, or . . . legitimate regulation' permit the employee's supervisor, co-workers, or the public to enter the employee's workspace. Further, employers can conduct 'reasonable' warrantless searches even if the searches violate an employee's reasonable expectation of privacy. Such searches include work-related, noninvestigatory intrusions (e.g., entering an employee's locked office to retrieve a file) and reasonable investigations into work-related misconduct.

The reasonable expectation of privacy test formulated by the O'Connor plurality asks whether a government employee's workspace is 'so open to fellow employees or to the public that no expectation of privacy is reasonable.' This standard differs significantly from the standard analysis applied in private workplaces. Whereas private-sector employees enjoy a reasonable expectation of privacy in their workspace unless the space is 'open to the world at large,' Government employees retain a reasonable expectation of privacy in the workplace only if a case-by-case inquiry into 'actual office practices and procedures' shows that it is reasonable for employees to expect that others will not enter their space. From a practical standpoint, then, public employees are less likely to retain a reasonable expectation of privacy against government searches at work than are private employees. Courts evaluating public employees' reasonable expectation of privacy in the wake of O'Connor have considered the following factors: whether the work area in question is assigned solely to the employee; whether others have access to the space; whether the nature of the employment requires a close working relationship with others; whether office regulations place employees on notice that certain areas are subject to search; and whether the property searched is public or private.

The courts have rejected claims of an expectation of privacy in an office when the employee knew or should have known that others could access the employee's workspace. In contrast, the courts have found that a search violates a public employee's reasonable expectation of privacy when the employee had no reason to expect that others would access the space searched. While agents must evaluate whether a public employee retains a reasonable expectation of privacy in the workplace on a case by case basis, official written employment policies can simplify the task dramatically. Courts have uniformly deferred to public employers' official policies that expressly authorize access to the employee's workspace, and have relied on such policies when ruling that the employee cannot retain a reasonable expectation of privacy in the workplace. Of course, whether a specific policy eliminates a reasonable expectation of privacy is a factual question. Employment policies that do not explicitly address employee privacy may prove insufficient to eliminate Fourth Amendment protection.

Written employment policies and 'banners' are particularly important in cases that consider whether government employees enjoy a reasonable expectation of privacy in government computers. Banners are written notices that greet users before they log on to a computer or computer network, and can inform users of the privacy rights that they do or do not retain in their use of the computer or network. In general, government employees who are notified that their employer has retained rights to access or inspect information stored on the employer's computers can have no reasonable expectation of privacy in the information stored there. For example, in United States v. Simons, computer specialists at a division of the Central Intelligence Agency learned that an employee named Mark Simons had been using his desktop computer at work to obtain pornography available on the Internet, in violation of CIA policy.

The computer specialists accessed Simons' computer remotely without a warrant, and obtained copies of over a thousands picture files that Simons had stored on his hard drive. Many of these picture files contained child pornography, which were turned over to law enforcement. When Simons filed a motion to suppress the fruits of the remote search of his hard drive, the Fourth Circuit held that the CIA division's official Internet usage policy eliminated any reasonable expectation of privacy that Simons might otherwise have in the copied files. The policy stated that the CIA division would 'periodically audit, inspect, and/or monitor [each] user's Internet access as deemed appropriate,' and that such auditing would be implemented 'to support identification, termination, and prosecution of unauthorized activity.' Simons did not deny that he was aware of the policy. In light of the policy, the Fourth Circuit held, Simons did not retain a reasonable expectation of privacy 'with regard to the record or fruits of his Internet use,' including the files he had downloaded.Other courts have agreed with the approach articulated in Simons and have held that banners and policies generally eliminate a reasonable expectation of privacy in contents stored in a government employee's network account.

Of course, whether a specific policy eliminates a reasonable expectation of privacy is a factual question. Agents and prosecutors must consider whether a given policy is sufficiently broad that it reasonably contemplates the search to be conducted.If the policy is narrow, it may not waive the government employee's reasonable expectation of privacy against the search that the government plans to execute. For example, in Simons, the Fourth Circuit concluded that although the CIA division's Internet usage policy eliminated Simons' reasonable expectation of privacy in the fruits of his Internet use, it did not eliminate his reasonable expectation of privacy in the physical confines of his office. Accordingly, the policy by itself was insufficient to justify a physical entry into Simons' office. In most circumstances, a warrant must be obtained before a government actor can conduct a search that violates an individual's reasonable expectation of privacy.

4

E-Commerce: Principles and Practices

Electronic commerce includes only transactions using Transmission Control Protocol/ Internet Protocol. Electronic commerce is thus seen simply as an Internet application. While the focus of attention and most growth projections are indeed on Internet-based electronic commerce, the two remain separate yet intersecting. This chapter has adopted the broader definition, viewing electronic commerce as encompassing both the Internet and closed networks, as well as hybrid networks.Total current use of electronic commerce, including the use of closed networks, and debit and credit cards, is measured in the trillions of dollars.

E-commerce encompasses three distinct types of transactions: those between businesses, those between businesses and consumers, and government services. These transactions are supported by the information technology infrastructure, consisting of hardware, software and enabling services. Transactions are not limited to purchases of goods and services, but move along a spectrum beginning with information gathering and exchange, progressing to negotiation and decision to purchase, finally to completion of transaction and after sales support.

In fact, at present, much of electronic commerce activity is concentrated in information gathering and exchange used to support purchase decisions. As electronic commerce grows, the importance of sales transacted on-line is expected to increase. Business-to-business applications are driving the growth of electronic commerce, accounting for about 80 percent of Internet-based electronic commerce. Businesses have used EDI for over 25 years to conduct transactions with suppliers. Now, lower costs and greater accessibility are causing businesses to move to the Internet, or to create hybrid networks through the use of intranets and extranets. In addition, an entirely new group of business users is coming on-line, mainly small and medium-sized firms that lack the resources required to support EDI.

Consumer use of the Internet is still in its infancy. A Commerce Net/Nielsen survey conducted in 1997 found that only about 16 percent of Internet users in Canada and the United States have made purchases over the Internet.As companies anticipate rapid growth in electronic commerce, significant investments are being made in the hardware, software and services required to support it. Global Internet-related investments were estimated to sum to about US$40 billion between 1995 and 1997, a portion of which was dedicated to electronic commerce. This US$40 billion in fact exceeded electronic commerce rev-enues. An entirely new cadre of network-based intermediaries is developing, providing information search and evaluation (e.g. search services, Web site evaluators), marketing, product and customer information, and secure on-line payment. Traditional sectors of advertising and delivery also play critical intermediary roles. The United States is estimated to account for about 80 percent of worldwide Internet commerce revenue, followed by Canada at 5 percent. The United States accounts for between 70 and 85 percent of the top 100 sites by category of Internet purchases (e.g. finance, shopping). Canada has the second highest number of top-100 sites. Many people are predicting that electronic commerce will become a pervasive form of business within the next ten years. Assessing how likely this is to happen requires an examination of the intrinsic advantages and challenges of electronic commerce in general, and of specific types of transactions.

E-commerce provides a powerful means of diffusing the advantages of networking throughout the economy, based on a platform provided by the information technology sector. This sector is strong and growing, as demonstrated by increasing shares of gross domestic product (GDP). In the United States, the information technology sector has grown from just under 5 percent of the economy in 1985 to just under 8 percent in 1997. Given that prices for information technology goods and services have fallen dramatically – for example, the cost of microprocessing computing power has fallen from US$230 to US$3.42 per MIPS (millions of instructions per second) since 1991 – this increasing share of GDP is even more impressive. The story is the same in Canada. The information and communications technology sector accounted for 5 percent of GDP in 1990, increasing to over 7 percent in 1996. This sector accounted for 30 percent of total economic growth between 1990 and 1996, with compound annual growth rates of 7.6 percent during this period, compared with 1.5 percent for the total economy. Electronic commerce will spur continuing growth in the information technology sector. Given its potential to change how business is done, electronic commerce will have even broader impacts, promising to accelerate growth not only in the information technology sector itself, but also across all sectors of the economy, such as manufacturing and retailing.

The intrinsic advantage of the Internet as a platform for electronic commerce rests on the open, non-proprietary nature of the network: the Internet allows businesses to use a global, interactive means of infrmation exchange at a low cost. While some would argue that such a capability already exists through existing communications networks such as telephone, fax or proprietary networks, the Internet offers an unmatchable combination of interactivity, versatility, low cost and speed. The implications of worldwide, low-cost information exchange are profound. The full potential of computerized design, manufacturing, delivery and services may now be realised by linking all parts of a distribution chain together, from product concept, design, testing, and manufacturing to marketing, after sales and service. For example, software designers and automotive manufacturers can test concepts and prototypes with users, and demand forecasts can be immediately passed from marketing to production and the supply chain. As a result, efficiency and productivity are increased through lower procurement costs, reduced processing errors, reduced inventories, and faster time to market. For example, by linking marketing to manufacturing and procurement, IBM improved inventory turns and experienced savings of US$500 million due to lower investment and operating costs. Automotive companies have reduced material flow to the supply chain from up to six to less than two weeks. Companies are also adopting the Internet as a base for business transactions to gain a competitive advantage, often at the insistence of other business partners in a supply chain. These forces are expected to result in the rapid growth of business-to-business electronic commerce.

From the consumer's perspective, electronic commerce offers significant benefits. Convenience, increased access to information, lower prices, and choice are benefits cited most often by consumers. For example, a small business, Unique Patterns Design of Halifax, Nova Scotia, is able to offer custom patterns that are tailor-made for each customer. Electronic commerce is also being used to support purchases made in conventional retail channels, as it allows consumers to gather information and comparison shop on-line.

Products and services most suited to electronic sale are those that are information intensive and can be delivered digitally, or tangible products that do not require tactile examination and can be easily shipped. Early leaders in consumer electronic commerce have fit this profile, most notably financial services, computer hardware and software, travel, entertainment, and books and CDs. Electronic commerce has widespread benefits beyond those related to the transaction of business. Governments at all levels are turning to the Internet as a means of increasing the range, reach and availability of their services. Services are available 24 hours a day, seven days a week, independent of location. The costs of providing these services can be significantly reduced for both users and governments. Electronic delivery of government services will also facilitate the future integration of government services from different departments and different levels of government. Other public sector institutions such as those in the education and health sectors are also using the Internet as an affordable tool to increase the reach of their services. Computer-based training can provide information which is immediately available and tailored to specific needs, making the goal of lifelong learning more attainable. In the health care sector, the Internet is being used to allow rural or remote doctors, clinics and hospitals to access specialized knowledge and services usually found only in urban centers, and to diffuse information to the public. Most broadly, networking promises to allow citizens to participate more fully in society and create new sense of community through greatly improved means of communications. The potential for electronic commerce is real. However, limiting factors exist, many based on the Internet itself, including issues of universal access, governance, and the future capacity of the underlying network.

Access to the Internet, while growing, is far from universal: in Canada, 36 percent of households own a personal computer, and 13 percent had Internet connections in 1997. If Internet access from home, work, school and elsewhere is included, access is just over 30 percent. The majority of large businesses and an estimated 43 percent of small businesses have Internet access. While these levels of access are among the best in the world, they do not come close to the near-universal penetration of established communications technologies such as the telephone.

Electronic commerce promises to transform the conduct of business, consumer and government transactions, offering the benefits of more efficient supply chains, greater convenience and choice, and lower cost of doing business. However, before these benefits are realised, businesses and consumers want to know that transactions are private and secure, that legal and financial frameworks exist to support transactions and that the information infrastructure works. Many possible scenarios exist for the future of electronic commerce. Optimists assume that these issues will be addressed and that electronic commerce will continue to grow. The contrary, pessimistic belief is that growth in electronic commerce, particularly growth in on-line sales, will stagnate as underlying problems remain unresolved, which could lead to a spin-drying of the Internet into smaller managed proprietary networks.

Electronic commerce promises to be a major generator of jobs and growth in the next century, through improvements in the productivity of business, growth in consumer transactions, and development of the supporting information technology infrastructure. Experience has shown that early leaders quickly establish market dominance. Those who enter first are able to help shape evolving rules as well as business and consumer behaviour. Canada enjoys many advantages that position it to compete effectively in electronic commerce. Canada has the highest standing of post-secondary education enrolment in the world, ranked first in knowledge workers by the World Economic Forum. Its telecommunications infrastructure is world class – it has among the lowest telephone costs in the world and the lowest Internet access charges among G-7 countries; it is second only to the United States in telephone mainlincs and Internet hosts per capita among G-7 countries; and it has many pioneering telecommunications and information technology companies that are recognized worldwide.Analysis of the challenges facing the use and growth of electronic commerce, reflecting views from business, consumers, provinces and territories, as well as international organizations, points to four key areas for electronic commerce action in Canada.

Most business relationships, whether between a consumer and a company or between firms, require a strong element of confidence and trust. The impersonal and remote nature of electronic commerce places a heavy burden on the need for means to reduce or eliminate risk. Security, privacy and consumer protection are all required to instill trust in electronic commerce, for both businesses and consumers. A body of rules that govern how business and government transactions are conducted has developed over time. To remove barriers to the use of electronic commerce, these rules need to be examined to assess how they apply to the digital world, and adapted where necessary, to create a level playing field which is predictable and consistent for all kinds of commerce.

Electronic commerce will not grow without a strong platform that includes network access and availability, and open standards.Electronic commerce is part of a broader process of economic, social and cultural change, characterized by the globalization of markets and the shift toward an economy based on knowledge and information. Opportunities for jobs and growth created by elec-tronic commerce need to be distributed as widely as possible among citizens, consumers and businesses, through development of skills and awareness, and government leadership as model users. The Canadian electronic commerce strategy is based on the recognition that the private sector has the key role in developing and expanding electronic commerce in Canada. Government's role is to provide a supportive and responsive policy environment for businesses and consumers, one that allows for market flexibility while ensuring a minimum baseline for a fair marketplace. Countries that can provide such environments will be better positioned to compete internationally. To this end, the Canadian government and private sector are working together to implement the Canadian electronic commerce strategy.

Electronic commerce is intrinsically global. The actions of any one country will have limited impact unless they are part of a larger international framework. Canada is not developing domestic policies in isolation, but is committed to working with other countries to develop the international frameworks necessary to make electronic commerce grow.

— *Organisation for Economic Co-operation and Development:* Canada's commitment to the international agenda is demonstrated by hosting the OECD Ministerial Conference on Electronic Commerce, in Ottawa, October 7-9, 1998. The conference includes governments and international organizations as well as business, labour and consumer interests. It leads to the establishment of agreements and action plans spelling out the current and future roles of government, international organizations and the private sector in addressing key electronic commerce issues. The Ministerial Conference represents the culmination of a series of electronic commerce conferences held by the OECD, beginning with a conference focussing on consumer views held in Paris in March 1997, followed by a conference focussing on business views held in Turku, Finland, in November 1997.

— *Asia Pacific Economic Cooperation:* In November 1997, APEC leaders agreed to the development of a work plan for electronic commerce. Under the direction of a task force co-chaired by Australia and Singapore, the first phase of the work plan – consisting of benchmarking electronic commerce developments in member countries – has been completed.

— The second phase of the program is being reviewed by leaders at their meeting in Kuala Lumpur in November 1998, including the development of an electronic commerce vision statement to promote the use of electronic commerce in the region, and the development of recommendations for technical cooperation and capacity building, public sector use of electronic commerce, and outreach programs targeted at small and medium-sized enterprises (SMEs).

— In addition to the Task Force, APEC Ministers of Telecommunications and Information Industries approved a reference framework for action to guide the work of telecommunications groups on a range of electronic commerce issues.

— *World Trade Organization:* Canada has also taken a leadership role in ensuring that the trade disciplines of the WTO apply to electronic commerce. At the second WTO Ministerial in May 1998, members agreed to launch a comprehensive study of the trade policy aspects of electronic commerce, with a view to providing recommendations to ministers for future actions by the third Ministerial in 1999.

— *Free Trade Agreement of the Americas (FTAA):* The FTAA has formed the Joint Government-Private Sector Committee of Experts on Electronic Commerce to make recommendations to ministers on how to increase and broaden the benefits of electronic commerce and, in particular, how electronic commerce should be dealt with in the context of FTAA negotiations. The committee is developing working guidelines and will be delivering recommendations for ministers prior to their October 1999 meeting.

— *G-8 Pilot Project: "A Global Market for SMEs":* The project, being coordinated by Japan, the United States and the European Commission, involves 20 countries and international organizations, including Canada. Its overall objective is to provide a framework and implementation plan for global coordination and cooperation in electronic commerce, focussing on SMEs.

Business and consumer transactions require assurances of trust – trust that transactions are secure and private, that transactions are supported by complete and accurate information, and that consumer redress is available. Measures developed for conventional commerce may be inadequate to provide trust in the digital economy. For example, while once data were held securely within an organization, either in paper-based files or in internal computer systems, now the Internet and hybrid forms such as extranets and intranets allow for potentially widespread information access. Issues of security once related only to law enforcement, not to protecting on-line transactions.

Government baselines exist for business and consumer protection, but key issues – such as the verification of the identity of parties and the determination of transaction jurisdictions within a global context – remain unaddressed. In addressing these issues, both governments and the private sector have a role. Governments can legislate or regulate, while looking to the private sector to introduce voluntary codes and develop technological solutions. Many of the elements of building trust involve both federal, provincial and territorial governments – the Uniform Law Conference of Canada, and the Consumer Measures Committee established under the Internal Trade Agreement, are pivotal in establishing model laws and providing guidance on consistent national approaches.

Secure electronic transactions can be provided through the use of cryptographic technologies and certification authorities. These authorities, by binding parties to their respective digital signatures, provide authentication as to the identity of the transacting parties. Cryptographic technologies also provide for the integrity and confidentiality of the messages that are exchanged, and ensure that neither party to the transaction can deny its participation in the exchange of information (otherwise known as non-repudiation). The benefits of cryptography for electronic commerce, privacy protection and crime prevention are clear. It is equally true that cryptographic technologies can be used to hide criminal activity and to threaten national security. Investigations, prosecutions, and the enforcement of laws and regulations could be hampered without lawful access to the evidence of illegal activity. Canada does not restrict the freedom of choice of individuals or businesses to import or use cryptography. Users are free to determine what kinds of authentication and encryption products and services they need. Canada controls the export of cryptography along with 32 other nations that are members of the Wassenaar Arrangement, which stipulates which products require export permits and which do not. Canadian cryptography policy is under review in order to ensure that it contributes to the realisation of Canada's goal to be a leader in the use of electronic commerce, and to ensure that it reflects an appropriate balance among business, human rights and privacy interests, public safety and law enforcement, and national security interests. The policy, released in the fall of 1998, provides greater certainty for the business community, more confidence for consumers and support for law enforcement and national security. The strategy for the protection of privacy is to put the Canadian Standards Association National Standard into effect through light legislation, complemented by private sector action and consumer awareness

The Government of Canada's fall 1998 private sector information privacy legislation strikes a balance between industry's interest in compiling and using personal information and the consumer's right to have personal information adequately protected. Consultations held during early 1998 found that there is strong support for using the Canadian Standards Association (CSA) Model Code for the Protection of Personal Information (also referred to as the CSA National Standard), as the basis for any such law, and the Office of the Privacy Commissioner of Canada as the oversight agency. There is also general agreement on the need for a consistent approach among federal and provincial privacy laws for the private sector. While to date, only Quebec has legislation, there is strong support for the use of the CSA Standard as the starting point for any new legislation.

Canada has led the world in developing a National Standard for the protection of privacy. This Standard, developed by businesses, consumers and governments, addresses the way organizations collect, use, disclose and protect information, and the way individuals access personal information.

An informed public is vital to the protection of personal information. Both the private sector and governments can work to raise awareness of privacy issues and ensure that citizens know their rights and the best way to protect their personal data. A good example is the partnership of the federal government and Stentor to fund a multimedia game, Privacy Playground: The First Adventure of the Three Little Cyberpigs, to raise privacy awareness among children.

Technologies such as cryptography, firewalls and screening devices can help protect personal information. The government encourages the development and use of such technologies for the lawful protection of its citizens. The Working Group on Consumers and Electronic Commerce, composed of consumer and business associations and governments, is finalizing Canadian guidelines on consumer protection in electronic commerce. The guidelines define consumer protection requirements and provide the basis for development of voluntary and legislative measures related to consumer information, contract formation, privacy, security and redress.

A range of consumer protection legislation already exists in Canada, in both provincial and federal spheres. The Consumer Measures Committee established under the Agreement on Internal Trade is considering ways to address consumer protection in electronic commerce. Consumer Protection Rights in Canada in the Context of Electronic Commerce, a report prepared by the legal firm of Gowling, Strathy & Henderson, is being used as a basis for discussion. The Government of Canada is also looking at provisions under the Competition Act governing deceptive trade practices and misleading advertising.

Governments, business and consumer groups agree that voluntary codes can play a vital role in areas not covered by legislation. For example, the Canadian Code of Practice for Consumer Debit Card Services, established in 1992 by consumer groups, businesses, and provincial and federal governments, has successfully guided consumer protection practices of financial institutions. The Working Group on Consumers and Electronic Commerce will be addressing consumer awareness in the guidelines on consumer protection in electronic commerce, including the need for consumers to be provided with advice on how to minimize the risks entailed in electronic transactions, and legal rights and obligations.

Technology can provide the tools to make information available to consumers. Examples include posting information on laws that apply in different jurisdictions, and posting seals of approval on Web sites that meet defined criteria (e.g. CA WebTrust). Consumer, business and government representatives have agreed that electronic commerce protection should be guided by principles of:

— *Media-neutrality*: Consumers should enjoy the same level of protection in on-line transactions as they do in other forms of commerce.

— *Harmonization*: Consistent frameworks can help Canadian consumers and businesses become early adopters of electronic commerce and attract business worldwide.

— *Consultative approach*: Consumer, public interest groups and governments will work together to define the right blend of voluntary and regulatory measures.

A body of rules that governs how business and government transactions are conducted has developed over time. These rules include legal and commercial frameworks, financial issues and taxation, and the protection of intellectual property. As new forms of business practice evolve, marketplace rules play a critical role in creating codes of conduct – for example in the use of electronic signatures, the assignment of liability, and the protection of trademarks. Without clear rules, the use and growth of electronic commerce will be stalled. The overriding need is to remove barriers to the use of electronic commerce by clarifying how these rules apply to the digital economy and updating them where necessary. The objective is to ensure that equivalent treatment is provided for digital and non-digital transactions in a consistent and predictable manner. Business has clearly stated that clarifying marketplace rules should be the government's top priority.

Consistency among and between provinces and territories and the federal government is critical, particularly for legal and commercial frameworks. The Uniform Law Conference of Canada (ULCC) is playing a leadership role in this regard. All government and business operations are subject to law. Law has traditionally presumed the presence of paper records – that presumption is no longer valid. As a result, the application of law to paperless transactions may lead to uncertain results. Governments are acting to make adjustments to laws to bring certainty to the use of technology.

Over 300 federal statutes contain provisions requiring documents to be "in writing" or equivalent words. Rather than have each department amend legislation piecemeal, the Government of Canada's fall

1998 electronic documents legislation allows departments to adopt a set of general provisions authorizing the use of electronic communications. Provinces and territories are being encouraged to undertake statutory reforms along similar lines, as set out in the Uniform Electronic Commerce Actapproved in principle by the ULCC in August 1998.

Many legal rules and the law of evidence assume the existence of paper, signed or original records. While most electronic records are, in practice, being admitted in litigation, the courts have struggled with the traditional rules of evidence with inconsistent results. The ULCC approved the Uniform Electronic Evidence Actin August 1998, which evaluates the integrity of an electronic record by considering evidence of the reliability of the record-keeping system that generated the record. The federal Department of Justice has proposed amending the Canada Evidence Act, to make it consistent with the ULCC Uniform Electronic Evidence Act. Provinces and territories will also consider amending their legislation to reflect the ULCC Uniform Evidence Act.

The challenge is to link the electronic signature to the person signing the electronic document. The Government of Canada is proposing that what makes an electronic signature trustworthy is the use of a reliable technology, such as digital signature technology, combined with a reliable certification authority (CA), such as those operating under the Government of Canada Public Key Infrastructure (GOC PKI) and those CAs that have cross-certification or are otherwise recognized by the GOC PKI.

Internet Service Providers and other Internet intermediaries have expressed concern about the possible extent of their liability with respect to areas covered by a number of federal and provincial laws – e.g. obscenity, copyright, consumer protection, fraud and defamation – which may result from actions of their clients. The uncertainty surrounding liability may be an impediment to investment in electronic commerce and to its pace of development. The OECD has reviewed legal frameworks applicable to content in its member countries. The Government of Canada has released for comment a study on Internet content-related liability and is currently analyzing the issue.

In the longer term, impacts on other aspects of legal frameworks such as corporate and competition laws will be of interest.The relationship between competition laws and intellectual property is discussed in section 2.3 Intellectual Property Protection.

The view of both Canadian and international taxation authorities has been that current tax systems and structures founded on basic principles of neutrality, fairness, certainty and simplicity will continue to be appropriate to address the changes brought about by electronic transactions. Attention has been focussed on ensuring that tax administration can keep up with changes in the market. The Minister of National Revenue's Advisory Committee on Electronic Commerce issued a report in April 1998 titled Electronic Commerce and Canada's Tax Administrationthat examines how existing taxation systems apply to electronic commerce. The report examines, among other issues, jurisdictional questions (e.g. the concept of a permanent residency), impacts of disintermediation (the splintering of intermediary services) on tax collection, and tax compliance. The Government of Canada's response to the report was released in the fall of 1998. Given the global reach of electronic commerce, most of these issues can only be dealt with in an international context. Canada is participating with other OECD member countries in developing international implementation strategies that will include the implications of electronic commerce on tax treaties, transfer pricing guidelines, the application of consumption taxes and customs duties and tariffs.

In May 1998, WTO members agreed to refrain from applying customs duties on the electronic products and services delivered electronically and to review this decision at the third WTO Ministerial meeting in 1999. A two-track approach, linking a comprehensive WTO work program on electronic commerce with a moratorium on customs duties, was based on a proposal submitted by Canada to the General Council in April 1998, and was later adopted by ministers of the QUAD (Canada, the U.S., the Commission of the European Union and Japan).

Financial firms are rapidly expanding their delivery channels, by using new communications technologies to broaden the geographic scope of their operations and obtain more convenient, cost-effective links with customers. Financial intermediaries, such as banks, credit unions, brokerages and insurance agencies, are supplementing personal branch banking with on-line services through the Internet, telephone networks and automated teller machines. Intermediaries are applying new digital technologies to reduce their cash-handling costs and simplify payment processing. With the help of new technology, specialized financial service providers are entering the sector, increasing competition and leading to the unbundling of services in certain markets. For example, brokers offering both trading and securities market information are now competing with on-line brokers who simply trade and provide no other services.

Changing delivery channels are intrinsically linked to opportunities to create new products and services. Technologies such as risk management tools, digital certification and cryptography create potential for new products such as automated sourcing of capital, on-line clearing and payment intermediaries, and information brokerage. Canada's financial institutions are involved in the development of new technology that may improve the efficiency of transactions and consumer convenience while helping to ensure privacy and the security of financial information.These changes are having an impact on the nature and structure of the Canadian financial services sector. The (MacKay) Task Force on the Future of the Canadian Financial Services Sector, which reported to the government in September 1998, made recommendations aimed at ensuring the sector's ability to meet global competitive challenges and the interests of consumers, and to take advantage of technological advances.

The global nature of electronic commerce also raises issues related to cross-border transactions in financial services. These issues are being examined by both national governments and international bodies such as the Basle Committee on Banking Supervision and the World Trade Organization. Intellectual property (IP) laws establish the rules for the ownership and use of key types of digital content central to the development of electronic commerce, such as music, computer programs, video and multimedia works. In addition to the need for clear rules on ownership and access to content, other key IP issues include liability of Internet intermediaries, trademarks and domain names, and database protection. New international agreements and other forms of cooperation are being considered to address these concerns, through the WIPO, the FTAA, APEC and the OECD. Canada is an active player in these discussions. Canada's national IP legislation is being reviewed to determine whether it needs to be adapted and whether it will be in Canada's interest to undertake any new international obligations.

WIPO member countries adopted two new treaties in December 1996, the WIPO Copyright Treaty and the WIPO Performances and Phonograms Treaty. These treaties give right-holders including authors, performers and record producers an exclusive right to make their works, performances and sound recordings available through interactive media on a demand basis. Canadian banks are partnering in the development of new electronic payment systems based on smart cards that allow consumers to purchase goods and services using prepaid electronic "value" in lieu of cash. The value is typically stored on an integrated circuit in a plastic card and can be read using special devices including point of sale terminals. Special encryption software helps ensure the security of the electronic value. Some electronic money systems allow for the transfer of value over communications networks as well as direct, person-to-person transfers. They also contain provisions with respect to copy protection and rights management information, among other new rights.Canada signed the WIPO treaties in December 1997, but has not yet ratified them. In July 1998, the government released two discussion papers that consider what, if any, amendments to the Canadian Copyright Actwould be necessary in order to comply with the treaties. Canada's copyright legislation, as amended in 1997, already provides a framework for copyright protection that is largely up-to-date compared with legislation in many countries.

The Canadian government is currently analyzing the issue of the liability of Internet intermediaries, such as Internet Service Providers, for intellectual property infringements, as part of its ongoing consultations on Internet content-related liability. WIPO is also considering certain aspects of liability, including applicable law and jurisdiction. Ongoing reform of the Canadian and international domain name systems (DNS) has highlighted the need to ensure that these systems and other Internet practices reflect IP rights and obligations appropriately, notably trade-marks. One major structural problem is that the Internet is international, whereas trade-marks law is national in scope. WIPO, with private sector input, has convened an international process to solicit recommendations on IP issues associated with the DNS. Progress on the reform of the Canadian DNS has also led to the recognition that a balanced approach is needed.In the context of increased availability of data through electronic means, databases are more and more important in a knowledge-based economy. Industry Canada and Canadian Heritage are engaging in a consultative process with major stakeholders to assess how Canadian laws apply to protection of databases, and whether a special form of IP protection should be developed for databases.

Global Rules of E-commerce

In order for electronic commerce to succeed on an international scale, a global framework that provides for privacy, cross-border dispute resolution and recognition of electronic contracts needs to be put in place, Carol Charles writes. She adds that the leaders of the G-8 industrial countries can play a key role in the creation of this framework. When the leaders of the Group of Eight (G-8) industrial countries convene their annual summit this July in Okinawa, Japan, they will be deliberating issues in an economy shaped by the rapid expansion of global electronic commerce. The value of worldwide business-to-business electronic commerce is projected to leap to $7,300,000 million in the year 2004, or about 7 percent of total global sales transactions, up from $145,000 million in 1999, according to a recent report by the Gartner Group, a worldwide business and technology research organization.

Global electronic commerce has led to profound changes in the way business is conducted. Networked organizations and decentralized corporate processes have changed relationships between the producers and users of goods and services, and spurred the rapid integration of global markets. Information and communication technologies and new developments such as online business-to-business exchanges and virtual trading networks have transformed traditional business practices by connecting critical business systems directly to key constituents like customers, employees, suppliers and distributors via the Internet. Examples are the united online marketplace for auto parts recently set up by General Motors Corporation, Ford Motor Company and Daimler Chrysler, and the online buying alliance between International Business Machines Corporation, Ariba and software developer, i2 Technologies Inc. These exchanges have reshaped the world of business and trade transactions. The private sector has been the driving force behind this phenomenon. A report issued by Forrester Research, a leading Internet research firm found that of the 80 U.S. firms they surveyed, 93 percent plan to buy and sell on the Internet in 2002.

The paradox remains, however, that while networked technologies are a great leveler of economic and social structures, they also have the potential to exacerbate the "digital divide" -- the gap between the level of e-commerce development in industrial countries and that in countries and organizations standing on the sidelines of the global e-commerce revolution. Internet-based business-to-business electronic commerce creates new market structures that enable business partners to switch allegiances at low cost, since the Internet expands choices and options to suppliers and consumers on an exponential basis. In addition, it enables contracting parties to exchange information, best practices and market feedback in real time.

Countries left out of the loop could experience the costs of severe economic isolation in this highly competitive environment. Recent findings by Computer Economics, an e-business adviser to corporations, suggest that while e-commerce will continue to boom in the next decade, Africa, South America and parts of Asia could be left out of the trade revolution. According to Computer Economics, just 6 percent of e-commerce will be transacted in these regions this year, and this figure will rise by only 1 percent by 2003. There is a very real possibility that developing countries may be constantly playing catch-up with the technologies and policy principles that have been formulated in the developed world. Also, the "digital divide" is hampering the ability of developing economies to be part of the ongoing process in developed economies: of assessing and possibly re-defining the existing rules for global electronic commerce. One of the key functions of the Global Information Infrastructure Commission (GIIC), an independent, non-governmental initiative launched during the G-7 summit meeting at Brussels in 1995, has been to ensure that developing countries are constantly engaged in this dialogue. Through its global network of private and public sector commissioners who represent both developed and developing countries, the GIIC has worked with national governments, industry groups, and international organizations - to advance the dialogue on the rules needed for the global information economy, as well as to create awareness and build constituencies for change.

In its work over the past five years, several factors have led the GIIC to conclude that the global networked economy needs increasingly flexible legislative solutions to the challenges posed by rapid technological change. These solutions must be formulated on the basis of international dialogue among various stakeholders in the information revolution, including the private sector, national governments, international organizations and consumer groups. These factors are:

Regulatory Frameworks in Constant Flux: The technological convergence of telecommunications and computers has revolutionized the way in which society produces, stores, and uses information. Meanwhile, the rapid growth of networks across national boundaries has blurred the lines between providers, suppliers, and originators of information. These developments have called into question how regulatory systems can ensure trust, confidence and consumer protection within a rapidly globalizing technological environment. For example, on-line issues related to digital copying and Internet domain names are raising critical issues about the ownership of copyrights and patents - and are creating brief and sometimes fluctuating values for intellectual property rights, privacy, and security, as information is digitally transformed and moves through its various iterations. The continued education of government regulators and consumers, as well as the development of technology-neutral self-regulatory schemes in partnership with the private sector, is essential to spur institutional adaptation and quick response to new technologies and applications.

New Definitions of Individual Rights: In this new networked economy, businesses can employ data integration technologies such as customer profiling to understand customer needs, provide support over the Internet, and integrate these customer demands within their supply chain. The use of these technologies is leading to increased awareness of what consumers perceive as potential violations of their rights as individuals, such as the misuse or usurpation of personal data, inaccurate and incomplete information and payment fraud. By the same token, the networked economy has put information and power back into the hands of the individual, with user communities being redefined in accordance with common interests rather than by geographical or physical proximity. In the electronic age, the buyer has access to information - and is thus empowered to change loyalty in an instant. So if businesses in the electronic age are to maintain customer loyalty and be competitive, they have to improve the service and value they bring to their customers.

Businesses recognize that it is in their best interests to protect the privacy of their customers, and to build trust and confidence that personal data are accurate and will not be misused. As a result, businesses are collaborating to develop self-regulatory codes of conduct, trustmarks, and seals to ensure flexible yet enforceable trust systems that are awarded to online retailers who comply with a high- and independently verifiable standard for electronic commerce. These seals cover every aspect of their operations, from their trading status to their privacy and security policy, customer service and support policy, information integrity, and warranty information. In its work in both developing and developed countries, the GIIC has observed that many countries do not have laws or cultural morés that support the preservation of personal privacy. We do not want to see the lack of a globally recognized framework for privacy protection lead to the establishment of data havens in which personal information is illegally traded or abused.

Challenges to Jurisdiction in Cyberspace: As transactions become more global, the control of government institutions over economic or other activity occurring in cyberspace is increasingly eroded. Jurisdiction and rules of origin are the two key factors impacting cross-border e-commerce, requiring that national and international frameworks be harmonized to enable dispute resolution and redress. Currently, issues relating to taxation, intellectual property, and consumer protection all depend on the rules of origin -or country of consumption. However, as transactions move online and become increasingly global, both business and consumers are becoming wary of the costs they may incur if they need to engage in cross-border litigation of their rights.

By using Alternate Dispute Resolution (ADR), consumers and merchants can settle their disputes through a trusted third party in a low-cost and speedy way. There are several examples of ADR, such as BBBOnLine, part of the Council of Better Business Bureaus in the United States, and Cybertribunal in Canada. Other organizations involved in international dispute settlement for electronic commerce are the ICC International Court of Arbitration of the International Chamber of Commerce (ICC), and the World Intellectual Property Organization's Internet-based WIPO-Net, which has been set up to arbitrate IP-related electronic commerce issues. However, to give businesses and consumers in global electronic commerce additional certainty, together with robust, reliable electronic commerce transactions, such certification efforts need to be extended to other countries and jurisdictions.

Authentication and Security: Authentication and security are critical for assuring people that they are transacting electronic commerce in an environment free from illegal attack or trespass. Strong, market-led encryption technologies are essential, as well as minimum necessary legal frameworks to authenticate electronic signatures. In addition, a legal framework must be in place to punish the dishonest. Since the private sector is leading in the area of encryption, there needs to be a partnership between the private sector and governments to create the frameworks necessary to ensure the trust and authentication needed to stem criminal activity. Since users tend to distrust government controls on encryption, governments should commit to removing all controls on cryptographic technologies and applications and should cooperate with businesses to facilitate the internationally secure exchange of information.

Universal Commercial Codes: Legal codes specifying commercial, contractual, and liability issues are the underpinnings of electronic commerce and are essential to building consumer confidence. As global electronic commerce expands, businesses are looking to a permanent framework for electronic commerce transactions that is also guaranteed and recognized by national governments. The 1996 Model Law of the United Nations Commission on International Trade Law (UNCITRAL) provides national legislators a technology-neutral framework of internationally acceptable rules to remove legal obstacles to e-commerce and creates a more secure legal electronic environment. The Model Law has been the basis for the development of e-commerce laws in Singapore, Korea, and Colombia, and has spurred the discussion of similar initiatives in Australia, Canada, Chile, France, Hong Kong, India, Slovenia, Brazil, Mexico, Morocco, New Zealand, Peru, the Philippines, Thailand and Tunisia. However, in spite of this activity, most countries have been slow to convert what has been the norm for commerce between parties for several centuries -- the exchange of paper documents -- into the electronic environment. Increased education and the involvement of the legal community within countries or trading blocs or regions such as Asia-Pacific Economic Cooperation and Free Trade Area of the Americas are critical to the rapid expansion of global electronic commerce and the involvement of additional countries.

The GIIC has been spurring the dialogue about removing barriers to electronic commerce in many countries around the world, including India, China, the Philippines and Venezuela, as well as many countries in Africa. In addition, the GIIC has worked in partnership with the Alliance of Global Business (AGB), a coalition of businesses in 140 countries, to urge governments to rely on business self-regulation and the voluntary use of empowering technologies to create trust across the spectrum of users and providers for e-commerce goods and services. Some initiatives include the AGB's 1999 Global Action Plan for Electronic Commerce, the Fact Sheet on the Duty-Free Treatment of Electronic Transmissions, and the Discussion Paper on Trade-Related Aspects of Electronic Commerce.

Most countries of the world - including the developed ones - are still only learning how various information technology innovations will affect the economy and labor markets. For developing countries, this process is far more profound, as governments and private sector groups endeavor to restructure their economies for the global digital economy.The G-8 representatives at the Okinawa summit have a unique and unprecedented opportunity to facilitate international cooperation for a secure global environment and a new international approach to building a global information economy in which every nation and every individual has a chance to participate.

Any global approach or framework needs to be flexible enough to support the growth of the information economy, encourage trade and investment flows, create jobs, and provide consumers with the benefits of competition, while encouraging a stable, secure environment for electronic transactions. Partnership with the private sector and international organizations such as World Intellectual Property Organization, the World Trade Organization, Organization for Economic Cooperation and Development and UNCITRAL is essential in creating cooperative systems to:

— Exchange information about best practices.

— Increase consumer satisfaction and confidence in doing business on the Internet.

— Establish merchant credibility and trustworthiness.

— Support and enhance the self-regulation of Internet commerce.

— Encourage the development of guidelines and symbols to support electronic commerce.

Finally, G-8 leaders need to extend these endeavors to provide technical and financial assistance to those nations on the sidelines of the global electronic commerce revolution and also to bring consumers and small and medium-sized enterprises in the dialogue. The inclusion of these actors can only serve to create a robust, secure, global information infrastructure, expand global trade and economic growth, and, most significantly, minimize the threat of an ever-widening digital divide.The Global Information Infrastructure Commission (GIIC) is a global forum of private sector and government leaders from the information and telecommunications industries who address policy decisions impacting the growth of the world's information networks. The work of the GIIC focuses on three main areas: global information infrastructure development, global electronic commerce, and education in the information age.

E-Commerce Guidelines

Consumers International set up a study, bringing together an international team to conduct an extensive practical research exercise, with the aim of determining where the real problems for consumers lie.Once consumers start buying from abroad, there are complex consumer protection issues to resolve—in particular, whose legislation they are covered by. International bodies are fully aware of the need for work in this area. The study of consumer shopping makes a number of recommendactions that will focus the energies of policy-makers, providing evidence that there are certain key consumer protection issues that must be addressed. Many specific recommendations arise from the detailed research findings. These are summarised below.

— If consumers are to take full advantage of the global shopping mall theoretically offered by the internet, they must feel confident of receiving a consistent standard of consumer protection wherever they shop In order to make this possible, a co-ordinated international approach is needed to the formulation of guidelines governing electronic commerce. National governments should be encouraged to adopt best practice guidelines developed at international level (eg by OECD).

— Because adherence to many aspects of best practice guidelines is voluntary, consumers need a way of recognising internet shops which offer high standards of consumer protection with ease, wherever in the world those shops are based. The development of an internationally recognised certification or labelling scheme, which indicates that shops meet agreed minimum standards on a range of key issues, would go a longway to offering this international reassurance.

— As online consumers experience many types of problem, such as nondelivery of goods or obstruction in obtaining refunds, so there is a need for a third-party redress mechanism that offers a further channel to the consumer retailer that offers a furtherchannel to the consumer once dead lock has been reached with the retailer. Such a mechanism needs to cover all companies selling goods to consumers on the internet. It needs to be accessible, affordable, fast, consumer-friendly, and binding on the company concerned. For such a mechanism to have teeth regardless of where a consumer shops, it must be supported by national governments.

Consumers must be provided with details of the retailer's identity and physical location. Consumers should be made aware of the full name of the company they are dealing with, as this may not always be the same as the web address. The Consumers must at least be provided with the retailer's geographic address, the country the company is registered in, a phone number, and an e-mail address. Where applicable, the consumer should also be given the registration number or licence number for the retailer, and contact information for the body with which the business is registered or authorised, to enable the consumer to check legitimacy. Sites should make it clear to the consumer which countries they deliver to, before the order process is embarked upon. This information should be clearly sign posted from the home page, and should be kept up to date. Sites must display one overall total price to the consumer before the order is completed, which should include any delivery charges. If sites are marketing to consumers in other countries, it is important that they design their sites with the facility to incorporate the delivery charge in the total price, once the consumer has provided the relevant information about where they live and what form of delivery they want. Delivery charges can make a significant difference to the overall cost, so it is not acceptable to ask the customer to contact the retailer separately to obtain delivery costs. Retailers supplying to other countries can also do much more to assist consumers in converting prices into their own currencies. Only one in four of the sites in other countries purchased from gave any assistance with converting prices (eg by providing a currency converter). This is not a difficult facility to provide, and helps the consumer considerably when deciding whether to make a purchase.

Terms and conditions contain essential information such as cancellation and cooling-off rights, payment and delivery terms, and dispute resolution, so it is essential that they be presented to the consumer before the purchase is completed. Retailers should design sites to ensure that purchasers are shown the terms and conditions before confirming their order, or are offered a link to click on to the terms and conditions before confirmation. Terms and conditions must be clearly sign posted/titled, and clearly differentiated from other information, so that consumers can identify that this is the legal part of the contract.

Terms and conditions should be provided in a manner that can be readily printed off and kept by the consumer for future reference. Consumers International and other consumer groups are firmly of the belief that the law governing internet transactions should be the law of the consumer's home country, in order that he or she is familiar with the protection available. This is a controversial area which is engendering much debate at present. Some retailers do stipulate within the contract which law they would like to apply, but a final decision on this, should a dispute arise, will be taken by the judge hearing the case. If a retailer specifies that the law governing transactions on its site is that of the retailer's own country, rather than the consumer's country of residence, that condition must behighlighted to the consumer in a clear and unambiguous manner.If a consumer agrees to such a contract, the consumer must not be deprived of the key consumer protections offered in his/her own country. Equivalent levels of protection must be offered. In addition, the consumer must have the right to pursue any dispute with in his/her own country of residence.Prior to the conclusion of the contract, the process of finalising the contract should be clearly explained to the consumer.

However, although access to the internet is growing all the time among individual consumers, they have been slower than businesses to explore the possibilities of buying products over the internet. Even in the United States, only 29% of the 53.5 million adults with internet access have made an online purchaseIn the United Kingdom, shopping ranks well below issues like education, business and e-mail access as reasons both for going online in the first place and for continuing to use the internet. The slow take-up of online shopping can be put down, at least in part, to a lack of confidence in buying through this new medium, and to fears about security and fraud. Although the study did not pick up any instances of fraud, it did reveal some grounds for consumers' lack of confidence. As the study reveals, when consumers commit themselves to a purchase online, they may not know the full identity of the retailer they are dealing with. They may not be told the terms and and conditions of the contract, or what their rights are when returning goods or obtaining redress. Nor may they have sufficient access to the retailer if something goes wrong – and the chance of something going wrong, such as non-delivery or damaged goods, is fairly high. If electronic commerce is here to stay, national authorities, consumer organisations and businesses all have an interest in building consumer confidence by ensuring that consumers have the necessary access, protection, and service standards when buying.

So much work is going on around the world on amending existing legislation and codes of practice, and on establishing new guidelines governing electronic commerce, that it would not be feasible to list all these initiatives here. The ones set out below are those which are most relevant to the consumer protection agenda.The World Trade Organisation (WTO) has established a work programme on electronic commerce (adopted by the General Council on 25 September 1998), and published a study (Electronic *Commerce and the role of the WTO, WTO* Publications, March 1998), which identifies a range of issues that need to betackled, including access to the internet, regulation of content, security and privacy questions, and the legal and regulatory framework. The Organisation for Economic Co-operation and Development (OECD) Committee on Consumer Policy is drafting guidelines (Guidelines for Consumer Protection in the Context *of Electronic Commerc*e), with detailed input from consumer representatives. The Transatlantic Consumer Dialogue (TACD) formulated recommendations on electronic commerce at a conference on 23-24 April 1999 in Brussels. These recommendations cover the establishment of minimum standards for consumer protection, urge the development of an International Convention on Privacy Protection, special protection for children, minimum standards for disclosure of information by suppliers, intellectual property rights, and call for discussion of a proposal to create a permanent global institution for consumer protection.The European Union's *Proposal for European Parliament* and Council Directive on certain legal aspects of electronic commerce in the internal market, *DGXIV, COM(98) 586 Draft,* seeks to clarify five issues where uncertainty arises due to divergent national legislation:

— place of establishment of service providers

— commercial communications (advertising, direct marketing etc) - definition and transparency requirements

— on-line conclusion of contracts

— liability of intermediaries

— implementation - strengthening enforcement mechanisms, facilitating the setting up of cross-border alternative dispute resolution systems, and a requirement for fast efficient legal redress in the on-line environment.

— The European Union's Distance Selling Directive, which is still in the process of being transposed into national legislation across the EU, is also highly relevant.

Many codes of practice are being developed around the world. These range from workbeing done by individual companies to guide lines that cover the practices of a particular industry (eg advertising or direct marketing) and guidelines that apply to businesses in general (eg Internet Service Providers' guidelines, BBB Online in the USA). These initiatives typically involve guidelines and/or certification, but they may also involve third-party dispute resolution. Consumer organisations in a few European countries, including the Consumers'

Association in the UK and Consumenten bondin the Netherlands, have recently launched a certification scheme which is run outside of the industry. Each participating consumer organisation provided information about what steps it and its government had taken on behalf of e-shoppers, and about the protection (if any) available for consumers making payment over the internet or wishing to return unsatisfactory goods.

Here we are going to outlines specific initiatives being taken to develop guidelines for electronic commerce in the countries included in the international consumer shopping survey. In addition to these specific guidelines, electronic transactions are of course governed, like any other transactions, by existing rules, for example on advertising, marketing, and unfair contract terms. However, agreement on which laws should apply in cross-border transactions has been the subject of debate. Countries within the European Union are currently in the process of transposing the Distance Selling Directive into national law. This will have an important effect on electronic commerce.

Australia: In *Consumer Protection in Electronic Commerce; Principles and Key Issues, April 1998,* the government National Advisory Council on Consumer Affairs set out 12 principles for electronic commerce:

1. Consumers using electronic commerce are entitled to at least the same levels of protection as is provided by the laws and practices that apply to existing forms of commerce.

2. Consumers should be able to establish the identity and location of businesses with which they deal.

3. Consumers should have readily available clear and

comprehensive information before and after any purchase of goods and/or services.

4. Sellers must state contract terms in clear, simple language.
5. Sellers should ensure they receive confirmed meaningful consent from consumers for a purchase of goods and/or services.
6. Consumers are entitled to receive clear information about the types of payment which will be accepted by the merchant or the payment provider.
7. Consumers are entitled to have their complaints and inquiries dealt with fairly and effectively.
8. Sellers should provide information to E-commerce guidelines and consumer rights: a country-by-country guide consumers about affordable and effective dispute resolution arrangements, when they are available.
9. Sellers must respect customer privacy.
10. Industry code administration bodies must closely monitor the application and effectiveness of their codes and be able to correct any deficiencies which are identified.
11. Each code-operating body should strive to maintain and promote consumer confidence in the global marketplace.
12. Governments should actively develop their consumer protection responsibilities. The Australian Consumers' Association magazine *Choice* has published a number of articles giving advice to consumers on electronic commerce.

Belgium: There are no specific guidelines for electronic commerce. The Belgian consumer organisation, Verbruikersunie, published guidance on electronic commerce in *Budget & Droits No* 138, April 1998.

Germany: There are no national guidelines for electronic commerce business practices yet. However, a 1997 law (Informations-und Kommunikationsdienste-Gesetz-IuKDG) covers electronic information and communication services, and contains consumer protection provisions in areas such as:

— identity of supplier

— data protection

— digital signatures and certification processes

— protection of children

— copyright.

The German consumer organisation, AgV, has published a number of studies and brochures giving advice to consumers on electronic commerce.

Japan: Effective approaches to consumer protection in electronic commerce (interim discussion of issues), Consumer Business Research Committee, Ministry of International Trade and *Industry, February 1998*, promotes the use of guidelines prepared by the Electronic commerce Promotion Council of Japan. These cover:

— consumer protection

— privacy and payment

— clarification of the law governing sales

— made in the home

— the need for strict enforcement of existing laws

— the need for greater education of consumers.

Sweden: The *Nordic Consumer Ombudsman's position paper* on trading and marketing on the Internet and in similar communication systems December 1998.

— marketing material

— clear provision of information

Throughout this survey Hong Kong is reffered rather than China, because the Hong Kong Consumer Council was one of the participating organisations, and because Hong Kong's consumer market remains distinct from that of the mainland.

— conclusion of contracts

— binding communications

— payment

— performance and complaints procedures

— use of e-mail

— processing of data

— marketing directed at children and young people.

United Kingdom: Various consultative documents have been issued by the Department of Trade and Industry. *Net benefit: the electronic commerce agenda for the UK* establishes some consumer and data protection principles, generally confirming that existing UK legislation covers internet transactions. The Office of Fair Trading issues extensive guidance to consumers on how to use the internet for shopping safely.

United States: The most important agency with

regard to consumer protection and electronic commerce is the Federal Trade Commission (FTC). The FTC's philosophy is that the laws, regulations and guidelines it governs are as applicable to online transactions as other transactions. Various documents such as *Advertising and Marketing* on the internet: The Rules of the Road and *Guide to Online Payments* illustrate this position. In addition, the FTC has held hearings to help it understand how traditional consumer protections can best be translated into the new medium. The one instance in which the FTC is moving in a new direction because of the internet is the privacy of children. In 1998 the United States Congress passed the Children's Online Privacy Protection Act.

One essential element of online shopping is the passing of credit card details to the retailer over the internet, and the associated worries about these details reaching unauthorised third parties. Although there are few rules specifically about credit cards and the internet, existing legislation is relevant in some countries. If the transaction involves a card and a Personal Identification Number, the Electronic Funds Transfer (EFT) Code says the consumer is liable for the first A$50 of any unauthorised transaction, unless the misuse stems from the consumer's negligence, in which case the consumer is liable for the total amount. If the transaction involved a card and no PIN, but does require a signature, the consumer is notable for any unauthorised transactions. Transactions involving a card and no PIN, not requiring a signature, are a grey area. Currently, some card issuers hold the merchant liable forum authorised transactions. This area needs to be clarified within the EFT Code, which is currently being revised.

5

Impacts of E-Commerce

E-commerce can be expected to bring significant productivity gains and higher economic growth resulting from the more efficient allocation of resources throughout the economy. Its impact is comparable to other micro-economic reforms and, like these reforms, the industry is taking a lead in implementing change across sectors.

Open access to the electronic marketplace for households as well as businesses, large and small, has only existed for the last three or four years yet it is growing quickly. It is already clear that e-commerce will bring significant changes to business, consumers, government and the economy. Companies are changing the way that they undertake their business. New industries are emerging and old ones are getting a new lease of life. Others may not fit in this new environment and may decline.

The net benefits will be realised if, as expected, widespread adoption of e-commerce proves to be a more efficient mode of doing business and the benefits exceed the costs. If this is the case, it could produce a growth dividend as a result of freeing resources that can be used in other parts of the economy.

The main sectors that expand are expected to be those that offer products and services that are amenable to e-commerce. This includes sectors such as media and entertainment, and banking and finance.

Some sectors will be larger because of flowon effects as changes ripple through the economy; housing is one example. Industry sectors that are essentially 'disintermediated' by the use of e-commerce may have lower output than otherwise. Industries involved in commodity exports may be sensitive to flow on impacts.

The efficiencies brought about by e-commerce are expected to result in changed employment opportunities. Some sectors will expand and increase job numbers, others will be smaller than otherwise. Overall, employment will expand.

Demand is likely to be strongest in occupations that are related to tourism and associated support services. It is possible that a flow on impact of the productivity gains and growth could be a temporary minor deterioration in the balance of trade. Looking into the medium term, the export enhancing benefits will outweigh other factors and the trade situation will improve. While all states are winners from the efficiency gains likely to be brought by e-commerce, some states are likely to benefit more than others. States that have a high reliance on commodity export activities will have to deal with larger offsetting costs.

The regions that benefit the most include country regions. Most country regions can expect a lift from the effect e-commerce has in compressing distance and making goods and services more accessible. Country areas that rely on tourism and related activities can expect an even larger boost. The regional analysis is obtained by disaggregating results that apply nationally. A different result may occur if regions adopted e-commerce at different rates. There is compelling evidence that the economy is in the midst of a major structural change. This chapter provides indications of the likely nature of changes that are in store and their flow on impact through the economy at large using quantitative measures where practical, recognising that information about the nature of the change that is underway is still fragmentary, taking Autsralias as a model.

It has combined the application of economic models based on theoretical frameworks with qualitative input from business leaders to form a rigorous and balanced approach that seeks to minimise the pitfalls inherent in each used in isolation. In Austarlia, industry input was obtained from an Industry Reference Group while the MONASH model was used as the framework for the main quantitative part of the analysis.

The Industry Reference Group (IRC) comprised of business leaders from selected industry sectors that were invited to join. All of the IRG members have considerable practical expertise and an understanding about the key strategic issues.

All hold responsibilities for the use of e-commerce in conducting their business, assessing its impact upon them, or advising about e-commerce issues in general. While drawing on IRG advice and input, decisions about the direct impacts, the nature of the flow on impacts and other findings remained the responsibility of the consulting team.

The MONASH model is a computable general equilibrium model of the Australian economy and provides a powerful tool for analysing structural change of this nature. Its use also imposes considerable discipline.

It requires analysts to concentrate on impacts that are measurable in much the same way as those impacts are measured in the national accounts. Most importantly, in using the model it is not possible to extrapolate growth beyond the underlying capacity of the economy to deliver it within likely resource constraints, just as the real world economy is subject to similar constraints.

Economic models are a simplification of reality. They are useful because they make it easier to understand the key drivers in the big picture without being distracted by the confusion of everyday life. Ultimately, not everything can be modelled. When modelling the impact of e-commerce it was important to trim and distil much of the detail to discern the main trends.

At its broadest, e-commerce is any type of business transaction or interaction in which the participants operate or transact business or conduct their trade electronically. Potentially this could include activities that include use of the telephone or the fax as well as the Internet. A broad definition would encompass activities long recognised under the label Electronic Data Interchange (EDI) as well as more recent developments in electronic transactions.

The general consensus is that at present, most e-commerce activity is at the business-to-business level. Business-to-consumer e-commerce is still in its formative stages of development. Consumers are still experimenting with the capacity of online purchases. It is also apparent that business-to-consumer sales face challenges.

There are some lingering barriers to greater use of online shopping. This includes concerns some consumers have about the security of personal information involved in transactions, uncertainty about vendor integrity, logistical bottlenecks, consumer protection, as well as general issues about access to the Internet.

It is likely that these issues will be managed over time largely through increased experience on the part of buyers, sellers and regulators. Addressing these and other issues has been a key thrust of government policy.

Activity that is widely considered to be e-commerce does not always end in a transaction. E-commerce has significant implications for the whole of business process. Adoption of e-commerce has led many organisations, for example, to reengineer the way that they do business. Others are transforming their approach to business, or their business model, entirely.

The speed of adoption of e-commerce is rapid. Many analysts see the fast rate as 'unprecedented'. While portraying a buoyant outlook, industry forecasts have consistently underestimated e-commerce growth. E-commerce activity is still quite small relative to the economy as a whole. Projections that e-commerce could reach a billion dollars or even many billions of dollars in turnover should be placed in perspective with the fact that economic activity in Australia involves final expenditure of over $550 billion and total transactions would be many times greater. It is perhaps more useful to look at e-commerce in comparison to other transaction types.

In the US, where e-commerce has been adopted more rapidly, the activity currently compares to direct marketing sales. Based on recent growth, however, online sales are expected to overtake those of direct marketing and amount to about half of credit card transactions within the medium term.

While there is a great deal of popular interest in the growth of e-commerce reflected in many media reports, it is difficult to obtain reliable data about this activity in Australia at present. This in part reflects the recent arrival of the activity and because companies' e-commerce plans are viewed as being strategic and therefore confidential. The data that is available points to rapid growth in the use of e-commerce here as elsewhere:

- At the end of 1998, there were 1.7 million Australians accessing the Internet at least once a week (regular users). This is projected to grow to 5.7 million by 2003. Adding email-only Internet users and casual users lifts the 2003 total to 10.9 million.
- Internet based commerce in Australia is predicted to grow from $61 million in 1997 to $1.3 billion in 2001.
- The number of business websites in Australia doubled between 1996 and 1998.
- There has been a doubling or better in annual revenues in recent years for several Australian companies that supply Internet systems or knowhow.

Growth in e-commerce infrastructure and support

Looking at the components of e-commerce activities there is general confidence that e-commerce support activities are growing rapidly.

Businesses are rapidly taking up e-commerce. The

number of companies active in e-commerce is set to explode in the next 15 months with a five-fold increase in active Internet trading sites.

Households appear to be continuing to increase their use of both the Internet and e commerce. Over 12 months from August 1998 to August 1999, the proportion of households accessing the Internet rose by 27 per cent to nearly 1.6 million households, or 23 per cent of all Australian households.

Meanwhile household numbers using the Internet as a means for paying bills and transferring funds are rising at a rapid rate. Many financial institutions are making investment in this area on the basis of this growth. In addition, purchases of both tangible and intangible products is increasing as individuals become more familiar with and trusting of security and authentication measures for conducting e-commerce over the Internet safely.

Huge estimates of the rapid growth in e-commerce sales generally do not impress economists. If US Internet retailers have boosted their sales to US$38 billion, so what? Economists will assume that this is offset by a US$38 billion loss by other retailers. Where is the net gain? Major economic issues include the following:

- Will e-commerce change productivity?
- Will it lead to new products and ways of doing things?
- Are there implications for employment?
- Will prices or the rate of inflation change?
- Is there a risk of industry dislocation?

- Will some regions be impacted more than others?
- What are the implications for international competitiveness?
- How will it change the way that business is done?

E-commerce is likely to have a profound impact on the economy at large. Even mainstream economic policy makers in other economies now recognise that the gains, characterised as productivity gains by macroeconomic analysts, are already having a substantial impact.

There are good reasons to expect that e-commerce can raise productivity. Firms can 'reengineer' to make maximal use of the capabilities of the new technology.

With a streamlined interface between production and sales, for example, firms could extend 'just in time' processes to almost every activity, reducing inventories and other input costs. They may also be able to streamline their own purchasing and orders processing systems and reduce the cost of finding and processing sales. E-commerce introduces potential distribution cost savings for many firms, particularly those that can digitise their products.

The productivity gains from investment in information oriented infrastructure has been a controversial issue amongst economists for some time.

It has been pointed out, for example, that the rapid adoption of information and communications technology from the mid-1970s onwards was accompanied by a slowdown in labour and capital productivity growth in most developed countries.

This led the Nobel-prize winning economist, Robert Solow, to observe in 1987 that 'you can see the computer age everywhere but in the productivity statistics'. The reasons for this may include the substitution of investment in information and communications technology for other types of capital and learning effects. These may mean that it takes time for business to realise the full benefit of new technologies.

While academic economists are still pondering the issues, practitioners are taking a more pragmatic approach. Alan Greenspan, the Chairman of the Federal Reserve Bank in the US, finds arguments that IT related productivity gains are ephemeral hard to believe. He gives every indication that he is taking the productivity enhancing e-commerce factor into account when forecasting economic outcomes and setting monetary policy. This was clear when he recently said that

'The Internet offers an admixture of potential new goods and services and potential lower costs of production. A major part of our current GDP reflects distribution cost, and it is evident that much of that is subject to potential competitive reduction through Internet marketing. I do not perceive the end of the shopping mall, if for no other reason than I have been strongly advised that shopping is not solely an economic phenomenon. But the relationship between businesses and consumers already is being changed by the expanding opportunities for e-commerce. The forces unleashed by the Internet may be even more potent within and among businesses, where uncertainties are being reduced by improving the quantity, the reliability, and the timeliness of information.

Following on from the potential for e-commerce to reduce the cost structure of firms, it will also change firms' relationships with their suppliers, or with their customers. This can change the structure of the complex interrelationships represented in value-added chains which make up the economy.

In the chain of activity between the producer and the final consumer, intermediaries perform many services including transportation, wholesaling and retailing—these activities are known as margins because their costs form a margin between buyers and sellers. In most OECD countries, margins typically add about 33 per cent to the final price of goods.

The use of e-commerce may also involve reintermediation. Making electronic purchases may involve inputs from new sources. This could include services provided by network services providers that both the buyer and the seller use to find each other.

Other new intermediaries may include electronic payment systems and services for authentication and certification of transactions. E-commerce may also involve some additional traditional inputs. Someone, for example, still has to deliver many of the physical products that are purchased. Generally, such services are far less labour intensive than the previous intermediaries, but nevertheless there is a cost.

Frictionless trade or trade with less friction? Initially it was supposed that e-commerce could lead to a 'frictionless' economy. This would be close to economists' text book world in which transaction costs essentially disappear, barriers to entry fall, geography becomes irrelevant and markets clear instantly. There have been many claims that the Internet represents a new 'frictionless market'. These claims have until now been largely based in theory, with little or no empirical evidence to substantiate the claims.

However, research released in August 1999 by Erik Brynjolfsson and Michael Smith at the MIT Sloan School of Management has produced evidence suggesting that prices for goods sold via the Internet are lower than at conventional outlets.

The MIT study compiled a data set of over 8 500 price observations collected over a period of 15 months, comparing pricing behaviour at 41 Internet and conventional retail outlets. It found that prices for books and CDs sold on the Internet average 9–16 per cent less than identical items sold through conventional channels.

While all Industry Reference Group members agreed that the reduced friction of Internet commerce would indeed reduce prices, identifying the extent to which it would reduce prices proved problematic. The results of the MIT study were therefore used as a benchmark against the observations of the Industry Reference Group to ensure that the direct impacts introduced to the model were in line with the most up-to-date analysis in this area. Evaluation of the economic implications of greater use of e-commerce requires understanding about developments within and between industries.

When discussing productivity and commerce with less friction, the tendency is to focus upon business efficiencies. Closer inspection reveals that there is another party—the consumer—in every transaction that is also concerned about ease, convenience and efficiency. Reducing consumers' transaction costs leads to efficiencies that free up resources (i.e. time) that can be used elsewhere.

With the Internet, businesses have greater scope to advertise and sell their products into a global market at lower cost. This is an opportunity that even small and medium sized businesses are taking advantage of already.

The impact of e-commerce will be magnified many times over when changes in capacity are reflected in completely new products and services. The impact of new products is particularly difficult to assess. It is possible that the future development of innovations based around greater use of e-commerce will follow the 'reverse product cycle' of innovation in services.

In the initial phase, incremental process innovations increase efficiency. In the second phase, more radical innovations lead to substantial improvements in quality. In the third, product rather than process innovations become important. It takes until this third stage for new industries and products to become dominant.

The combination of reduced production costs and increased competition over the Internet will have a significant downward pressure on prices and inflation. The Internet is severely curtailing retailers' pricing power by giving consumers the means to compare different offerings with the click of a mouse.

This phenomenon is not limited to firms who compete for business online. Competitive pressures affect competitors who remain off-line. Traditional off-line suppliers were forced to improve efficiency as they sought cost-effective ways to match the value propositions offered by their online competitors.

The translation to lower prices is not automatic with a number of quantitative studies finding that the evidence is mixed. The 'sticker price' of a good or service being sold using two different 'channels' may not give the full picture. Even where the price is the same, the cost of obtaining a product from the Internet is likely to be lower because it involves more convenience and less cost for the consumer. Studies that do not take this into account may be misleading. Certainly when looking at evaluations of the economic impacts of e-commerce, the full cost comparison should be factored in.

Many of the productivity improvements that greater use of e-commerce may bring also pose a threat to employment. Disintermediating layers of economic activity between buyers and sellers results in bypassing jobs. An offsetting factor would be that the lower prices for goods and services would stimulate demand in other areas and increase the demand for labour. Identifying the net impact requires an economy-wide framework. Not all labour is homogeneous.

Increased demand for skilled IT workers is unlikely to able to be met quickly by large numbers of recently retrenched shop assistants. Examination of the labour market outcomes would be enhanced through looking at changes in the economy's demand for people with different skills and occupations.

If greater use of e-commerce has an uneven effect on industries, affecting some more than others, reflecting differing geographic distribution of industries, regions are also going to enjoy differing benefits and costs. This also requires an economy-wide perspective to evaluate.

E-commerce may change the way that business is conducted and organisations are structured. E-commerce is likely to have an impact on transaction costs throughout the economy. Many transaction costs result at their core from limitations in information or in moving goods and services to where they are useful, among many other factors. Greater use of e-commerce appears to make it easier for buyers and sellers to learn more about products and prices, or to transport some items reducing transaction costs. Transactions costs are one of the key factors that define the boundaries between what activity is undertaken within a firm or a business, and what is essentially outsourced through purchases in a market. Thus firms rarely outsource strategic management, or key production functions.

Many firms are prepared, however, to outsource a sales function or logistical facilities by essentially selling their output to retailers or other intermediaries. If there is a major change in transaction costs, the boundaries between firms, industries and markets are likely to change in turn. It will be important when looking at specific industries to try to identify ways in which business models are changing. In general, e-commerce seems to offer the prospect of moving economic activity closer to some of the ideals of perfect competition: low transaction costs, low barriers to entry, and improved access to information for the consumer. It may significantly lower prices while improving quality. In doing so, e-commerce may significantly improve the efficiency of economies, enhance their competitiveness, improve the allocation of resources and increase long-term growth.

In Austalia, the Industry Reference Group (IRG) provided strategic input to help define the parameters to be used in the MONASH Model and provided comments throughout the process. This was important in giving the model a more realistic perspective. IRG members were requested to consider the most probable impacts of e-commerce on their industry sector, as well as ways in which value would be added to, subtracted from or transferred between sectors as a result of e-commerce.

A key enabler of e-commerce, demand for IT is expected by industry representatives to grow commensurately with the rapid rates expected in e-commerce. Exponential growth in computing power will unlock further applications of e-commerce. Widespread access to computers has been both a prerequisite for broadbased e-commerce activity and a driver of change.

Access to e-commerce is increasingly less dependent upon owning a sophisticated, full function desktop computer. IT products, such as software and hardware, are increasingly being sold via means that bypass traditional intermediaries. This sector can be expected to continue to receive a shift in consumer preferences towards purchase of its products.

Communications is a major input sector to e-commerce. Access to affordable bandwidth is unlikely to be a major constraint in future to all but a minority. New demands will alter inputs required and allow intermediaries to be bypassed.

New technologies, such as Wireless Access Protocol (WAP) will have a large impact on the future conduct of e-commerce. Similar to IT, communications industry representatives see this sector as enjoying a greater share of final and intermediate demand as a result of greater use of e-commerce.

An information-intensive industry with an established IT infrastructure, this sector will be able to extract greater efficiencies and bypass. traditional cost structures, such as the branch structure. Banks are looking at ways to expand their value proposition by linking new services to their existing customer base. Greater use of e-commerce in these activities could reduce bricks and mortar costs, especially for banks in terms of less need for expensive branch networks, and for labour and other inputs.

This sector is comprised of a range of professional 'knowledge' services that will benefit from greater efficiencies in dealing with suppliers and clients through electronic service delivery. Some traditional cost structures will be altered.

New products and services will be created, such as legal authorisation of electronic documents or data registry services. Media and entertainment A high profile industry, online forms of media and entertainment will compete with traditional forms for audiences, customers and advertising revenue.

A beneficiary of major productivity gains from previous forms of e-commerce such as EDI, manufacturing may extract further efficiencies made possible through open networks. Companies can build stronger relationships directly with customers including by selling products directly online. It is expected that many manufactured products will benefit from reduced retail and wholesale margins as a portion of these costs are disintermediated.

Traditional retail faces increased competition from online competitors with more effective product ranges and cost structures. It risks being bypassed to varying degrees by consumers making online purchases directly from producers or new infomediaries, especially in digital products and commodities such as CDs.

Improvements in supply chains will generate efficiencies and possible disintermediation in the transport sector. Transport stands to secure significant productivity gains from e-commerce. Greater productivity may also lead to decreased demand for labour. Additional value can be built into customer relationships, such as Qantas' frequent flier points website, or the 70 per cent of tickets sales that are e-tickets. Transport activities are conservatively expected to be able to save up to five per cent of their existing staff requirements over the next decade through more efficient administrative processes .

Significant efficiencies stand to be made in pharmaceutical supply chains. New service modes and channels to the consumer will be developed, as will expanding electronic modes of operation, such as telemedicine.

Considerable potential gains in terms of reduced 'avoidable incidents' were also identified although still difficult to quantify at this stage. No direct impacts are identified at this time in this sector in the interests of producing a conservative estimate of the impact of e-commerce.

E-commerce will provide greater opportunities for distance education and improved efficiencies through online processes to bypass traditional administrative functions.

Greater reliance on e-commerce is an increasingly unavoidable requirement when seeking to conduct educational services over multiple campuses, through distance learning, and to attract foreign students.

A high reliance on accurate information and large distances between producers and customers makes this sector conducive to the benefits of e-commerce.

E-commerce provides additional opportunities to generate operational efficiencies such as obtaining better weather and stock information or bypassing intermediaries and locating cheaper inputs. It also allows agribusinesses to market products more effectively to wider audiences. It seems likely that much of the savings to be experienced by the agriculture sector will be due to efficiencies in other sectors from which it buys its inputs.

Drawing the above impacts, it is possible to discern some broadly applicable impacts on business. Many of these relate to challenges that individual business are increasingly going to have to come to terms with. They do not generally impact on the overall level of activity or industry costs, and so will not be factored in to the modelling process that follows, but they should nevertheless be factors of increasing importance in the strategic thinking in business for some time to come.

The first of such findings is that industry representatives see that e-commerce is altering business models and, in particular, spheres of competition. Businesses are being forced to reassess who their competitors are in an online world as often they differ from their traditional competitors. There may be large new markets for some, but increasing competition is also a feature of the new environment.

Secondly, e-commerce is forcing business to rethink customer relationships. Industry representatives have broadly identified that e-commerce is making it possible for businesses to approach customers directly, whether for direct sales or product information and feedback, rather than going through intermediaries.

Order and delivery of products is being improved by e-commerce. Customers can be served from their home or business rather than having to go to a point of purchase. When products or services are digital or 'virtual', the entire process can be conducted electronically. While real goods still require eventual delivery, the process of gathering information, browsing, comparing and ordering can still be more convenient than by traditional means. A key theme that industry representatives reported was that e-commerce is being used to improve supply chain management. E-commerce continues the process of substituting information for inventories and reducing substantially the investment in warehouses. It continues to cut back the need for paper-based documentation and improves the speed of communication.

Some industry representatives have commented on the capacity for e-commerce to improve customer power by expanding their information base, particularly with respect to price differentials. As the Internet overcomes problems associated with buying products from a distance, alternative lower-cost suppliers can be found across a larger geographic range, widening the effective market and intensifying competitive pressures.

E-commerce is expected to allow competitors in other industries and other countries to enter markets as it bypasses the need for investment in local facilities. This has been seen in financial services, with the entrance of new dot.com players. Import competition is patchy with some sectors facing more competition than others. The simulation results that follow compare the expected outcomes with greater use of e-commerce against those that would have been obtained anyway, if use of e-commerce stayed largely static (the base case). The key inputs of the base case are:

- The economy will grow and exhibit changes in prices and industry composition in line with standard economic forecasts.

- Trends in world commodity prices.
- Trends in technology particularly as reflected in changes in input-output ratios for differing industries.
- Known policy changes of significance including issues.
- Immigration and population growth.
- Pre-existing trends in the use of e-commerce.
- The economic impacts of greater use of some forms of e-commerce. It is viewed that these developments continue well established trends, further developments are likely to happen anyway and they have been factored in to the forecasts about expected economic outcomes.

To evaluate the economy-wide implications of e-commerce, the analysis draws on 14 sets of direct changes to the Australian economy.

These changes are often referred to as 'shocks' because they change the balance that would have resulted without change. They cover four broad categories:

- retail and wholesale trade changes;
- selected sectoral changes;
- international trade related changes; and
- reintermediation costs.

If a shock saves ten per cent of an industry's labour and the industry's labour represents five per cent of GDP, then the direct GDP effect is 0.5 per cent. This recognizes that the shock releases resources that can be used to generate a 0.5 per cent increase in GDP.

The direct effect on public and private consumption is also noted for each set of shocks. This can be considered an indicator of the welfare effect of the shocks.

Composition and pattern of growth Real GDP increases as there are progressive increases in the extent of adoption of e-commerce in the economy at large. Three broad factors shape the composition of growth. Firstly, the economy makes better use of existing capital and labour. In economic terms there is an increase in total factor productivity. This technological change accounts for the majority of the increase in growth.

Secondly, more capital is invested in the economy raising the availability of this factor of production. The capital stock increases because the productivity gains brought about by greater use of e-commerce increase wage rates relative to capital rental rates. This occurs with a lag as investors react cautiously to changes in rates of return and the change is gradual. In the long run it is expected that rates of return will return to levels that would prevail without an e-commerce impact. Although additional capital inflows and investment are associated with productivity gains, and are largest when those gains are being enjoyed, the expansion in the economy also leads to a sustained increase in investment. It is assumed the additional capital is sourced from abroad through foreign savings and investment. These factors have implications for changes in the exchange rate.

Thirdly, there is an increase in the supply of labour, another factor of production. This stems from time savings for producers and consumers. Higher activity is sustained even after the full effect of the modelled e-commerce changes have taken place after a decade. In fact real GDP continues to rise slightly. This reflects dynamic benefits. E-commerce will be used intensively in the fastest growing parts of the economy. This means that the technological improvements become progressively more important.

Greater use of e-commerce is expected to generate increases in real wages and employment. Initially, real wages are fixed and employment adjusts to changes introduced by e-commerce. As more use is made of e-commerce, activity in the economy and employment will rise over time. Real wages eventually also rise.

In the longer term, the increase in employment declines somewhat because of higher real wages, but it remains above the base case forecast reflecting the increased supply of labour associated with the technological change. While job numbers may rise or fall in specific industries, the net effect is an increase in employment. The increase in real wages is a benefit of the expected structural change. It is part of the means by which employees obtain a share of the productivity gains. The increase in real wages could be brought about in one of two ways. One way would be through reductions in prices below their forecast path.

This would involve wages staying on their forecast path and producers passing on the efficiency gains as reductions in their prices. It seems more realistic, however, to expect that the Reserve Bank will preserve its medium term objective of keeping underlying inflation to within 2–3 per cent and allow real wages to rise than expect it to permit prices to fall below its target band.

To assess the welfare significance of the change, the increase in activity is translated into an increase in real consumption that it allows. Real consumption is a primary purpose of economic activity and is a better measure of welfare or material wellbeing than GDP.

While there are many factors which shape welfare outcomes, including environmental factors and others that are not always reflected comprehensively in the national accounts, all else being equal, most people would consider themselves better off with an increase in their ability to consume.

One step in the conversion of the results from changes in activity to consumption is to note that income is influenced by changes in the terms of trade.15. As part of the economic expansion generated by the greater use of e-commerce, export volumes expand. Despite this, it is likely that e-commerce will increase the prices of exports relative to imports.

Greater use of e-commerce would contribute significantly or disproportionately to greater environmental degradation or higher crime rates or other negative factors that would reduce welfare gains from increased consumption. In order to produce conservativeresults it is assumed that e-commerce does not alter the overall fiscal balance and therefore change the aggregate consumption rate.

That is, governments do not raise or lower tax rates, although the level of spending rises and falls with changes in the overall level of activity consumption relative to economic activity. Offsetting this to some extent, owners of foreign capital remit their after tax return on investment, generating a leakage to the domestic economy and reducing its consumption potential.

Greater use of e-commerce can be expected to lead to significant changes in external competitiveness. A key factor is that the real exchange rate is driven by changes in investment. The capital inflow that stems from the opportunities created by greater use of e-commerce pushes the value of the Australian dollar up.

In the longer term, when the investment pressure slackens (i.e. after 2007) the exchange rate moves closer to the base line projections. It does not fall back to the base case because e-commerce has a favourable long term impact on the terms of trade. The terms of trade improve because Australia will earn higher unit prices on a slightly smaller volume of exports. Additionally, the prices of imported items will fall relative to exports.

The appreciation of the real exchange rate is expected to have a significant impact on aggregate export and import volumes. The overall result is a deterioration in the balance of trade at first. This is gradually unwound as exports recover strongly when the exchange rate moves towards base case levels. The impact of these changes is not felt evenly through the economy. Tourism and related services exports enjoy a significant boost as a result of these factors. Commodity exports face offsetting disadvantages.

Changes in import and export volumes are measured by making a weighted average of the percentage change in the quantities of each individual commodity (e.g. wool, wheat). These weights are value shares.

Greater use of e-commerce results in structural change of the economy. It is expected to stimulate activity and employment in industries that benefit from increased awareness of their products or services, meet the growing e-commerce needs of other institutions or just grow through the productivity enhanced expansion of activity at large.

The majority of industries are expected to expand for one or more of the above reasons. The flip side of structural change is that some industries will experience some displacement. Naturally those industries that provide services that can be disintermediated by greater use of e-commerce face particular challenges.

They are likely to see less activity than otherwise, although they may still grow in absolute terms. Other sectors may be disadvantaged by the macro economic impacts identified earlier. Export oriented activities that are sensitive to changes in the appreciations in the exchange rate are particularly at risk.

Some industries are not directly impacted by e-commerce in the modelling exercise, but are affected nonetheless by the flow on effects that reverberate through the economy. Flow on effects positively impact some sectors. Increases in productivity and real wages have dual effects of freeing up additional investment and improving consumer confidence, both of which positively impact, for example, upon construction and ownership of dwellings. Additional economic activity generates greater government revenue and the public sector expends in line with activity at large.

Many of the industries in cluster two, however, are not affected positively. Real appreciation of the exchange rate negatively impacts upon many commodity sectors, such as mining, metal products as well as import competing sectors. Commodity exports become relatively more expensive abroad and others face greater competition domestically from relatively cheaper imported goods. The exchange rate appreciation is caused by real wage increases that arise from e-commerce related productivity gains in the rest of the economy.

Many of the export commodity sectors recover as the real exchange rate eventually returns towards the base case trajectory. This is the case for basic metal products and chemicals. The exception is mining. This largely reflects a sustained decline for black coal. Relative to other major mining activities black coal spends very little on intermediate inputs and therefore obtains no benefit from e-commerce while other sectors do.

Black coal accounts for an increasing proportion of mining activity at large in the base case forecast and so the sector at large sustains a contraction. In the agriculture sector, industries producing export commodities perform poorly relative to industries producing food for the domestic market or inputs used in emerging export products. This is because,exports are harmed by real appreciation. Agriculture recovers strongly following abatement in the appreciation of the exchange rate.

The structural change in the composition of Australia's industry brought about by greater use of e-commerce will also change the demand for people with differing occupational skills and experience. One person's labour is not a perfect substitute for another's in areas where skills matter. Retraining the workforce to better match the skill profile required by industry is a key requirement of smooth structural change.

The Australian MONASH model includes a module that allows analysis of changes in demand for differing occupations. It is important to note that this focuses on changes in demand. Labour is assumed to be able to move freely between occupations in the core MONASH model. The results cannot be read as indicating that educational systems will be able to meet the demand or indicate where bottlenecks may be experienced. Results for 340 occupations are available.

Changes stem from a mixture of direct effects and flow on impacts in industries that at first glance would seem to be quite removed from e-commerce. In contrast perhaps to a view that e-commerce is an IT issue leading largely to increased demand for computing professionals, the occupations expected to see large increases in demand are spread broadly. The occupations with the highest increases are associated with hotels, restaurants, entertainment and air travel. These are the industries that will benefit from an e-commerce related expansion of tourism. In addition, there is a varying degree of increased demand for professionals in health, education, business, finance, accounting and law. These benefit from e-commerce efficiencies.

The greater use of e-commerce in the industry will lead to an increase in demand for computing professionals above those already factored in to the base case. This is by no means the largest area of occupational demand. Occupations that experience a decline in demand for their services are in areas such as printing, retailing, ground transport and banking staff. Printing and retailing were identified as losing industries reflecting e-commerce related savings in paper used and savings of retail margins. Employment in transport is reduced by e-commerce related labour-saving technical change.

The flow on impacts that are forecast to result if the economy makes greater use of e-commerce in the way modelled should be viewed as being fairly robust. They should apply whatever cyclical changes the economy will in fact experience in the years ahead. If growth slows down, or accelerates, and is different from outcomes foreshadowed in the base case in this analysis, the forecast deviations could still be anticipated.

6

E-Banks and Financial Sectors

The economic role of the banking and financial services sector is to mobilise funds between savers and investors. The sector includes financial intermediaries and financial markets. Financial intermediaries include the deposit taking banks, building societies and credit unions, insurance companies and superannuation funds. The sector also includes value that is added by market institutions. Overall, the market environment in the banking and financial services sector is becoming increasingly competitive.

As imperfections in the operation of markets have receded with the development of new transactions technology and new ways of harnessing information, trade in markets has increasingly substituted financial intermediation. It seems that further change is ahead with the new capacities introduced by the use of e-commerce. The banking and finance sector was one of the first industry sectors to benefit from the use of information technology more generally.

Early computers were used for scientific and military purposes, not for commerce. The banking and finance sector has been a rapid adopter of e-commerce. The sector displays many characteristics that will facilitate the adoption and extension of e-commerce activities, such as the importance of product over location, many of its key services are easily virtualised, and great importance is placed on quick response times.

For some time now most of the transactions between banks in the payments system have been undertaken electronically. Banking systems have also progressively automated deposit taking and payments. Key developments have included the now widespread acceptance and utilisation of ATMs and EFTPOS. Use of Internet banking is also growing rapidly. Of the 1.7 million Australians using the Internet regularly, nearly 150 000 are involved in Internet banking. This is a threefold increase from a year ago. Internet consultancy www.consult projects that there will be about 270 000 Internet banking users by the beginning of 2 000. Most users are expected to extend their existing banking relationships.

While the four big domestic banks have Internet-banking offerings, the Commonwealth Bank is the largest. Forty five per cent of regular Internet banking users bank online with the Commonwealth Bank and nearly 30 per cent with Westpac. National Australia Bank is Australia's biggest banker to small business. Users of NAB Internet Banking, are reported to have increased from 8 000 to 26 000 in two months and are signing up at twice the rate of personal customers.

The key attributes that the commercial banks offer in their Internet banking facilities typically include:

- review transaction details;
- transfer funds between accounts;
- pay bills;
- transaction records and account statements;
- buying or selling of funds that can be used in other e-commerce sites;
- communicate securely with the bank;
- standard fees, or sometimes, lower banking fees per transaction; and
- customer convenience in terms of 24 hours a day, seven days a week service, without queues and from the comfort of one's home or office.

The National Australia Bank includes a 'pay anyone' feature in its Internet service which enables customers to transfer funds to accounts at other banks, a function that is not widely available on Internet based systems in Australia. Statistics from the US give an indication of why people use Internet banking and why they do not.

Financial markets

Financial markets have also been quick to adopt e-commerce and electronic trading. The Australian Stock Exchange (ASX) introduced the Stock Exchange Automated Trades System (SEATS) in 1987. Trading floors were abolished in 1990 and all trading was conducted electronically on SEATS. In 1994 the ASX introduced electronic and clearing settlement (CHESS). Reflecting continued use of e-commerce techniques, by 1999 settlement time was reduced to the trade date plus three business days.

Since the arrival of open access systems using the Internet, ordinary investors have also been quick to buy and sell shares electronically. Many new purely online brokers have emerged offering very low fees and several full service brokers have responded by offering online trading facilities of their own. Over 15 per cent of households in the US are reported to have conducted equity trades online. This compares with less than five per cent that bank online.

Most of what the ASX does is e-commerce, for example electronic trading of shares and executions has been occurring for 12 years. Given this history, the ASX believe that further creation of value from e-commerce will be due to increases in speed. For example, gross settlements now take three days, but they are gearing up to handle real time settlements. In that respect it will be a new product for the ASX, and will also change the risk characteristics of trades. There is also value added by the speed of the transaction as the value of the trade can change while it is taking place.

The ASX is also working with the NASDAQ to allow the joint buying and selling of shares on their indexes. Currently, if an Australian wants to trade with NASDAQ they have to find a broker with a US affiliate or contact a broker in the US. The funds for the trade have to be raised separately. When the new service is in place, the sale of shares on one index can be used to fund the purchase of shares on the other. This service will also allow the ASX to use its IT infrastructure more intensely. Re-intermediation could also occur, with brand name labelling of shares and finance. Quicken in the US is trying to provide bundling via a portal to banks, brokers, insurance and more. The seamlessness of any new service will be important. Another factor is that new players do not have commitments to existing players that existing players have amongst themselves. The business elements of e-commerce will evolve slowly–the ASX has need of digital certification and increased reliability.

Banks are keen to make greater use of Internet banking for many reasons, but a key factor is the substantial cost advantage this activity enjoys. The Commonwealth Bank states in its 1998 Annual Report that 72 per cent of all banking transactions are conducted through electronic channels, such as telephone, the Internet, ATMs, and EFTPOS terminals. Similarly, Westpac states that around 80 per cent of their transactions are done electronically. The National Australia Bank have recently reduced the percentage of transactions through branches from 19 per cent to 14 per cent. Every customer that is to switch from a branch transaction to a lower cost channel results in a substantial saving. Competition will force the banks to pass these savings on to customers as lower fees and prices.

Using the Internet for bill payment can provide savings to all parties involved including the merchant, customer and the bank. Electronic billing is likely to be a significant growth area in the economy in 2000.

A flow on impact of greater use of the electronic channels and consolidation in general has been the reduction in staff required. The following graph indicates the change in employee numbers of the four Australian major banks. It is important to note that these employee numbers include those added through domestic and international acquisitions by these banks.

In order to obtain the cost savings offered by the Internet, the banking and finance sector is buying significant volumes of IT inputs. It seems likely that the major banks have raised their IT spending to accommodate a major upgrade of e-commerce requirements. It is not clear if they intend to raise spending above these levels or merely to sustain them, or indeed, if the new capital expenditure round is now complete. In order to compete in the Internet market, banks and other financial sector firms must ensure that consumers are aware of their presence in this new context. The financial sector is the biggest spender on Internet advertising in Australia, nearly a quarter of the total spent coming from the sector. Five of the top-ten online advertisers in 1998 were from the financial services industry.

The traditional concept of a branch offering all services is also changing. Banks are setting up specialist transaction centres and centres that target specific audiences. The National Australia Bank (NAB) has 219 specialist business centres in addition to its 903 traditional branches and in Australia. The ANZ has a Business Direct Centre that offers lower priced products for smaller business with simple lending and financial service needs.

There is a trend toward the use of mobile lenders and investment advisers. Westpac have 1 000 mobile staff and during a 12 month period the Commonwealth Bank's mobile bankers conducted almost 50 000 home loan interviews, and over 24 per cent of all Commonwealth home loan approvals were generated by mobile bankers.

The Commonwealth Bank has traditionally used Post Offices to provide additional branch type services for their customers. The Commonwealth plans to extend this with Woolworths Ezy Banking Westpac is working with rural communities and introducing in-store branches in pharmacies, general stores and newsagencies.

Banks have traditionally provided an intermediary service of matching deposits with funding for loans. E-commerce provides an opportunity for banks to be disintermediated from this activity. The direct provision of loans by non-banking entities such as superannuation organisations and insurance companies could be an indication of this disintermediation. Calculated from information provided in the annual reports of the National Australia Bank, Commonwealth Bank of Australia, Westpac and the Australian and New Zealand Banking Group Limited. The data does not separate out increases in branches obtained through acquisitions of overseas activities, so probably understates the fall in branches used in Australia.

Traditionally banks have played an important role in the payment approval process. The trend towards the use of credit cards (versus cheques) has had (and still does have) the potential to reduce the role of banks in the payment loop. Banks have retained some control in this area to date as the card issuing body. The move towards SET in the online payment areas will re-intermediate banks back into the online payment approval process.

The likely acceptance of some form of digital cash in the future could potentially disintermediate banks again from the payment approval process. Elimination of value is also possible in the sector. Banks now act as intermediaries in matching depositors with funds to loan applications. The function could move to brokered markets, and even to a direct market. With payments, the provision of EFTPOS enabling payments was a valuable service to bank customers. Now with services such as

Telstra's SureLink, the payment service is provided as part of a larger service. This commoditises the pure payment service.

Greater use of e-commerce is also opening new opportunities in this sector. Regulatory reform, competition and the potential of the new technologies are breaking down distinctions between the roles that companies in the banking and finance sector play. E-commerce over the Internet has enabled banks to move into stock trading. The Commonwealth Bank's ComSec is a predominantly online share trading service, although it does provide a supporting telephone service. The ANZ has recently announced an alliance with E*TRADE Australia for ANZ customers to trade securities online. There is a trend for banks to offer complete financial services to individuals and organisations. This typically includes investment advice, insurance, superannuation, share trading, and funds management.

E-commerce is creating new value in the banking and finance sector. E-commerce assists organisations in becoming virtual CFOs for small businesses by handling all financial services and providing accounts receivable and payable services. The aim is to provide a full service from operational through to strategic. For consumers, the concept is to package services around 'life events' and to provide focussed advice and services. Internally, e-commerce is moving processes from the bank to the customer, for example instead of a loan officer completing an application in a face-to-face interview, the customer completes a form on the web.

Banks are also looking to take advantage of the collection of information to tailor their services and improve their marketing. The NAB announced in their

1998 annual report the development of a sophisticated information-based system that identifies customers with specific financial service needs. Called National Leads, the system provides high quality data and strong customer calling opportunities.

Internet banks

There is a trend in the US for the development of pure Internet banks—banks whose primary communication channel with customers is the Internet. Internet banks are able to design their business without wasteful and lower value 'bricks and mortar' assets and liabilities. They may have a 'second mover advantage' because they do not have to face the cost of restructuring.

There is evidence that they are able to offer financial services at prices well below traditional firms. This has not had an impact in the Australian banking industry at present. This may be because the traditional banks still offered a wider range of services that customers considered safe or perhaps reflect the fact that Australia's major banks have been quick to develop their own relatively sophisticated online banking functionality.

The Commonwealth Bank was online in December 1995 and had Internet Banking in February 1997. Nevertheless, traditional banking approaches are increasingly under competitive pressure. Relationship marketing is becoming more difficult as more organisations enter the market. Banking and finance institutions now face competition from online trading organisations that gain a complete picture of a consumer's financial relationships by building around the equity holdings and into banking, insurance, superannuation, etc. This can lead to an unbundling and rebundling of services.

Bill-paying over the Internet is likely to become business-as-usual within just a few years. The Gartner Group predicts that in two years virtually all banks will offer online bill payment, and industry analysts believe that Internet portals such as America Online (AOL) and Yahoo! will soon be offering online payment under their own brands. AOL's Rob Shenk says, 'A lot of people have stock portfolios, but everyone has a checking account. So it's a much more elemental service.'

A reluctance on the part of customers to switch to new providers may make sense: good financial relationships should not be thrown away for the sake of small short– term savings.

The growth of Internet banking and new competitors does not imply the end of traditional banks or financial services brokers. Reflecting existing strengths and consumer awareness, it may be a matter of changes in roles and involvement at different levels. One example of the transfer of value from the industry is the bundling of financial services as part of another transaction, e.g. buying a car, or factory equipment.

The finance can be provided or facilitated by a party other than one from the industry, distancing banking and finance from their customers, or replacing them. However, if banking and finance take a higher view of their role, using a business event model this opens opportunities for creating value and improving relationships using e-commerce in ways which it would be too expensive to do face-to-face. There are issues here of who has the 'right' or credibility to provide the service, i.e. who bundles whom. The transfer of value occurs if the service that brokers offer is unbundled. Brokers currently offer advice, risk management and execution. Risk management could be unbundled to the insurance sector, or new participants could enter using e-commerce services.

Banks from smaller countries in Scandinavia and Europe have been very aggressive in penetrating larger European markets with an Internet banking presence. Is there a scope for entry of banks from abroad into Australia using a similar strategy? There is no evidence to indicate that there has been a significant transfer of value to overseas firms through widespread offshore banking or other financial transactions.

In contrast, there is anecdotal evidence to indicate that despite falling transaction costs and improved information, many investors find overseas investment or deposit in overseas banks to be too risky. Industry sources indicate however that there is some scope for migration of this service, albeit over time.

The inflow of value from overseas is not significant and would be predominantly from the acquisition of international banking operations by the Australian banks and any associated movement of functions to Australia. For example The Bank of New Zealand owned by NAB operates its Internet site and undertakes all its processing in Australia including monitoring and supporting its ATM network. E-commerce is a major enabler of this, specifically EDI, the Internet and other dedicated networking systems.

The opportunities opened up by e-commerce is a factor driving change in the banking and financial services sector. Use of e-commerce is shifting demand and supply in the sector to lower cost more convenient service delivery channels. In meeting the broad range of financial service needs that customers have within a single entity, the distinction between banks and other traditional financial service roles is becoming blurred. The potential of online financial services has reduced many barriers to entry and is increasing competitive pressures. It is likely that cost savings that will result from this process will be passed on to consumers. When looking at quantitative analysis of the sector it seems reasonable to factor in a wide range of direct changes:

- direct labour savings extending the staff reductions the sector is already achieving;
- banking is also expected to be able to disintermediate other input costs, particularly those that relate to the operation of branch networks. To reflect this it can be assumed that a small reduction in inputs of construction and paper products is achieved;
- reflecting the increased convenience of online banking and financial services, time savings should be included as an efficiency gain for other industries that use the services of the sector as well as households;
- the sector has already boosted expenditure to purchase e-commerce inputs and these are already factored in to the base case forecasts.
- for the moment it is assumed that this sector will not face greater international competition or experience a significant boost in exports from e-commerce.

The IT industries are relatively new and dynamic in nature. The IT industries have a number of unusual characteristics. They are among the fastest growing industries. Technological change is rapid and product life cycles are short. Most product and service prices are falling rather than rising. Convergence in the industries is leading to the increasing inter-relation and interdependence of computing, communications and the media. This is also profoundly changing the structure and dynamics of the IT industries. Change in the IT industries and their capacity is driving change in the use of e-commerce while the IT industries are also being driven by changes in e-commerce usage.

The IT industries extend through a value chain including electronics to computing and telecommunications platforms, office equipment and consumer electronics, telecommunications carriage and services, IT services and to information and entertainment services.

Computing power has been doubling every 18 months for the past 30 years. At the same time, the average price of a transistor has fallen by six orders of magnitude, due to microprocessor development. In just six years, the cost of microprocessor computing power decreased from $230 to $3.42 per MIPS. No other manufactured item has decreased in cost so far, so fast. Whether traded or non-traded, the IT industries are growing strongly at a rate in excess of ten per cent per annum. It is estimated that approximately 500 000 Australians are employed by, or spend a substantial part of their time engaged in the commercial activities of the information industries.

Official statistics indicate that use of IT in Australia by the private sector is high: companies employing 100 or more people are almost fully computerised; 50 per cent of smaller companies are computerised and this rate is growing.Use of e-commerce by the IT industries The IT industries have been rapid adopters of e-commerce technologies and business models. The biggest advances in this sector have been in business-to-business e-commerce. More use is being made of e-commerce to facilitate the purchase of goods and services by consumers, but it is still very much behind the magnitude of sales made between businesses.

The greater use of e-commerce in the sector has the potential to add value or reduce costs in the following areas:

- value chain disintermediation;
- enhancing value in sales and after sales support activities; and
- improved operations.

There are many areas where greater use of e-commerce can bypass costs. The IT industry is now able to deliver many of its products using e-commerce. Items such as software and documentation that traditionally had to be shipped can now be delivered online.

Hardware is also becoming upgradeable without the need to physically replace parts. Software can be delivered online to allow customers to upgrade hardware such as modem cards. In general, there are many areas where businesses in the IT industries or their customers are using e-commerce to reduce supply chain costs, or enhance their convenience.

Warehousing, inventory and the volume of product in the cycle are much less than would otherwise be. This has also reduced the real estate required to store the inventory. The number of suppliers has been reduced, Cisco now tends to deal with the original manufacturer and manufacturers of components. The additional suppliers added time to the process and also forced Cisco to be a manufacturer. In some cases, Cisco has eliminated its own involvement. The other major elimination that has occurred is in the number of trips provided by the transport sector, now that many deliveries take place directly from the supplier to the customer.

Cisco builds virtually all its products to order, so there are very few off-the-shelf products. Before the company established an Internet sales capability, ordering a product could be complicated. Generally, an engineer at the customer site knew what type of product was needed and how it should be configured.

The engineer communicated this information to his procurement department who then created the purchase order and sent it to Cisco via fax, phone or email. A Cisco customer service administrator entered the order into Cisco's system. If the order went through 'clean', it would be booked and production scheduled within 24 hours. Nearly one out of four orders didn't get a 'clean' bill of health, however. Instead, when Cisco's system tried to validate the order, it discovered an error in how the product was configured. The 'dirty' order would be rejected, the customer contacted and the procurement cycle would begin again.

In July 1996, Cisco rolled out its web-based ordering and configuring system. Today, that same engineer can sit down at a PC, configure the product online, know immediately if there are any errors and route the order to the procurement department.

Because the customer's pricing structure is already programmed into the Cisco site, the authorised purchaser can complete the order with a few keystrokes. And, rather than calling Cisco to find out the status of the order, invoice or account information, a customer with the proper authorisation can access the information directly on the website. With the online pricing and configuration tools, about 98 per cent of the orders go through the system the first time, saving time both at Cisco and the customer's site.

Lead times have dropped two to three days, and customers' productivity has increased an average of 20 per cent per order. E-commerce is now fundamental to Cisco. Eighty per cent of orders in Australia are generated by e-commerce, up from 40 per cent three years ago. The objective is to grow the orders received electronically to 90 per cent next year.

Cisco's business is $400 million in Australia and $12 billion worldwide. As well as the benefits to Cisco, this use of e-commerce impacts on a lot of businesses that buy from Cisco. The use of online ordering has reduced the headcount in the order entry department by one in the last two years, although the volume of orders received has tripled. The quality of order entry has also improved, due to online checking at the time of entry, from a 30 per cent error rate to less than two per cent. Customers can also check delivery schedules online.

The whole process is more profitable, and better for customers. Orders are faster, cleaner, are checked against the manufacturing cycle, while more orders can be processed using fewer people. Customer satisfaction has increased from 3.5 to four, with five being a perfect score.

The users of the system, Cisco's customers, are medium to large businesses. Cisco does not sell direct to consumers. Cisco is also working on supply chain management, aiming and succeeding in being a 'virtual organisation'. Suppliers provide components, such as chips and boards.

Cisco demands that suppliers be online. This has eliminated complex processes, and made a tighter link to manufacturers with no middlemen. Effectively, 50 per cent of the physical boxes are delivered to the customer direct from Cisco's supplier. Cisco has an Intranet used by employees and suppliers alike. Suppliers access the same forecasting information as Cisco. Eighty to 85 per cent of software is now downloaded by customers, whereas it was previously distributed by CD-ROM. It used to cost $125 to send a CD, downloads cost $5. This has also eliminated the deliveries of CDs.

All product information, including technical information is available online. Eighty per cent of technical information is now sourced online by customers. Customers can also enrol for seminars online. This has achieved the objective of increasing customer satisfaction, while saving on the cost of distributing physical documentation.

Internally, expense accounts are submitted online and profiled automatically. Payments are made by direct credit to the employee's bank account. This system is used by all 18 000 employees worldwide. Cisco hopes to have invoicing online soon. The main benefits to Cisco of e-commerce have been the reduced head count, reduced inventory, reduced paperwork, and reduced direct costs such as with the downloading of software.

IT industries will also have to purchase more electronic inputs from new intermediaries in order to engage in greater e-commerce. The indications are that these costs will be relatively modest, certainly in proportion to the potential efficiency gains that IT industries are likely to obtain. The use of e-commerce is also increasing the complexity of the information technology requirements. Many organisations are outsourcing the management of their information technology systems. There is a transfer of value into the IT sector brought in by the outsourcing of IT and services from other industries, such as government, finance and travel.

Greater use of e-commerce is likely to drive changes in the way that business is done in the IT industries. It appears that there will be swings transferring value between activities in the IT industries. The first is the potential transfer from hardware to software—this is predominantly caused by the rapid reductions in costs of hardware while software has maintained its value. E-commerce has not been a major driver of this. There is a transfer from commodity manufacture to mass customisation. This has also resulted in a transfer in value from whole items to components. This is being driven by the varied nature of e-commerce and the many applications for the use of information technology in this area, resulting in the need to customise hardware.

For value creation there are very strong possibilities in many sectors, particularly in government. There are cost saving and productivity improvements possible from the use of e-commerce. The opportunity to create value is also high in IT services. IBM believe that software and especially services will be the drivers for growth, while the value creation in hardware is lessening. This means a transfer of value within the IT sector from hardware to software and services. This transfer of value is leading to a move from commodity manufacture to mass customisation, particularly for large customers, and the management of the assembly. The trend to network computing is leading to the value being held in the network not on the hard drive of the computer. One of the issues for all industries today, is how a business becomes an e-business. That is, not only setting firms up online, but helping them to deal with customers online, and integration into their existing systems and processes. IBM has used it own experience to assist its customers.

The process of convergence is also reshaping what it is that businesses in the IT industries will offer in future. Some companies that have been established in the industry for some time have responded dramatically to challenges and opportunities raised by e-commerce. IBM is in the IT sector, but also heavily involved in the e-commerce sector. The IT sector is a key facilitator for e-commerce, and will be one of the big winners.

Some in Australia focus on creating the hardware sides of IT and e-commerce in Australian (chip and other hardware manufacture) but IBM does not see enough critical mass in Australia to support these hardware efforts. Rather, IBM believes that Australia's opportunities are in services and content development which have a much higher value add.

The value proposition in the e-commerce world is different than for many other industries. In manufacturing, automotive for example, a basic model car is developed as the lowest common denominator, then features are added to add value. In e-commerce, the 'lowest common denominator' is the high end or perfect product, from which features are removed to subtract value. The model is more akin to book publishing, where the hardcover is published, and some time later a cheaper paperback is released. Time is also a driver of value, for example the latest stock prices on websites are available at a higher cost than those whose publication is delayed.

The growth of e-commerce internationally has led to a huge demand for high quality IT personnel. Many international countries are willing to pay quality IT personnel more than Australian companies. This is particularly the case with start-up IT companies. The transfer of value to or from overseas can occur with the rise of the Internet and network computing, with the offering of remote services, for example, remote education, application development, etc. The direction of the service flow will determine the direction of the value transfer, i.e. whether Australia positions to provide remote education services, or is the recipient of them.

Australia has some advantages over other countries that are resulting in an inflow of value from overseas. These advantages include:

- well educated and technically competent workforce;
- well positioned for Asian markets;
- large number of staff with multilingual skills; and
- globally located to support international call centres working on around the clock.

The Communications services sector is made up of telecommunications services, postal services and courier services. E-commerce appears to be having mixed effects in the sector. While telecommunications companies are big players in the e-commerce marketplace, postal and courier services are generally viewed as risking having their value being eroded as more information is shifted electronically rather than in physical form.

E-commerce is having a remarkable impact on the communications industry. Telecommunications carriers have an obvious role to play in providing the communication lines and bandwidth to make network access and ultimately e-commerce possible. Of major importance for telecommunications carriers is the impact of increasing data traffic and the use of the Internet for voice traffic.

The impact of e-commerce on communications is not restricted to the telecommunication companies. Postal services are also being impacted by e-commerce.

One might expect that as the sole supplier of traditional regular mail services in Australia, Australia Post would suffer a decline in the demand for its services as a result of increasing use of e-commerce. However quite the opposite has occurred— the number of items carried by Australia Post grew by 3.4 per cent last year from 4.3 billion to 4.5 billion. Even so, Australia Post is undertaking a number of strategies to find a fulfilling role in an environment of greater use of e-commerce.

Australia Post is expected to launch its Internet Fulfilment System (IFS) shortly, which will move beyond simple delivery to include electronic integration of its warehousing, distribution and track and tracing capabilities for online retailers. Australia Post already delivers an average of 22 000 items from Amazon.com every monthand is the largest delivery network to 8.5 million households and businesses in Australia. IFS will enable it to compete effectively for the increased delivery of Internet-ordered products as traffic grows into the future. In addition, Australia Post will launch a web-based bill presentation and payment system, which it expects to grow to 20 million transactions by 2003 (Note: Through its network of post offices, Australia Post currently handles around 170 million bill payments annually). Unlike online banking bill payments systems, Australia Post will offer bill presentment and will give customers the option to pay bills using accounts from more than one financial institution. Australia Post will not charge customers for using the services, instead it will charge billing principals for using the system. Consumers can pre-register with bank details and relevant information and an account ore credit card can be debited with a single mouse click.

Use of the Internet for billings, particularly for business-to-business transactions, is less expensive and more timely than traditional paper billings that use postal and courier services. The trend in electronic billings is expected to continue due to reduced transaction costs and improved service, and a greater insistence on the part of large businesses that suppliers be linked into their e-commerce systems.

Use of the Internet also offers cost savings from the standardisation of technologies that have historically been incompatible, for example, for fax transmission, broadcasting and telephone circuits, though opportunities for some functions are presently constrained by bandwidth limitations.

A cost saving for business generally that may affect telecommunications businesses is increased use of the Internet for selling at the expense of telephone selling and call centres. Automated selling is likely to require less labour for the selling process and for delivering after sales services, which is likely to consist of manuals and databases accessible to consumers over the Internet, with perhaps a small team of people on hand to solve difficult problems. Communications companies themselves, particularly postal and courier services, are also reducing costs as users of e-commerce services. E-commerce in the procurement of machinery and equipment was projected to compress wholesalers' margins by 25–30 per cent over the period under consideration. Also e-commerce would increase competition and more sophisticated competition would put downward pressure on the producer's prices.

E-commerce was thought to be pretty fully implemented in supply areas like fuel, so little further impact was projected. People noted that there were conflicting trends on fuel utilisation arising from e-commerce—greater customisation meant more frequent deliveries of smaller loads, so possibly increased costs, but computer assisted routing meant that the effect was small.

Telecommunications companies in the sector are incurring costs in creating new products. They are moving into e-commerce and application development and finding new value. They are moving more into Internet Protocols and data transmission. This is opening up a whole lot of new opportunities for them, especially in developing applications to suit different customer requirements, in this new environment that can mean developing software.

Communications sector companies are becoming involved in new areas of business, enabled by e-commerce and new technologies. Underpinning these lines of business are new technologies. A new technology which should have a big impact on the sector, and on business in general, is mobile e-commerce based on Wireless Access Protocol (WAP). Internet phones and Internet payment devices will also impact. One of the drivers of e-commerce is the availability of Internet devices. People are using Personal Digital Assistants more, and tapping into the existing mobile base depends on the right applications.

The impact of e-commerce is different for the two main industries which comprise this sector. The telecommunications companies are big players in the e-commerce marketplace, providing many of the products and services on which e-commerce is based, as well as moving up the value chain to provide e-commerce services directly. Telecommunications companies are also acting as re-intermediators and disintermediaters in setting up electronic marketplaces. Postal and courier services are seeing traditional markets erode but, at the same time, new markets evolving.

7

Executing Computer Searches

Computer searches differ from other searches because computer technologies frequently force agents to execute computer searches in nontraditional ways. Searches for computer files tend to be more complicated. Because computer files consist of electrical impulses that can be stored on the head of a pin and moved around the world in an instant, agents may not know where computer files are stored, or in what form. Files may be stored on a floppy diskette, on a hidden directory in a suspect's laptop, or on a remote server located thousands of miles away. The files may be encrypted, misleadingly titled, stored in unusual file formats, or commingled with millions of unrelated, innocuous, and even statutorily protected files. As a result of these uncertainties, agents cannot simply establish probable cause, describe the files they need, and then 'go' and 'retrieve' the data. Instead they must understand the technical limits of different search techniques, plan the search carefully, and then draft the warrant in a manner that authorizes the agents to take necessary steps to obtain the evidence they need.

Computer searches may be executed in a variety of ways. Some possibilities are:

— Search the computer and print out a hard copy of particular files at that time

— Search the computer and make an electronic copy of particular files at that time

— Create a mirror-image electronic copy of the entire storage device on-site, and then later recreate a working copy of the storage device off-site for review

— Seize the equipment, remove it from the premises, and review its contents off-site.

Searching computers with a warrant is as much an art as a science. In general, however, agents and prosecutors have found that they can maximize the likelihood of a successful search and seizure by following these four steps:

a) Assemble a team consisting of the case agent, the prosecutor, and a technical expert as far in advance of the search as possible. Although the lead investigating agent is the central figure in most searches, computer searches generally require a team with three important players: the agent, the prosecutor, and a technical specialist with expertise in computers and computer forensics. In most computer searches, the case agent organizes and directs the search, learns as much as possible about the computers to be searched, and writes the affidavit establishing probable cause. The technical specialist explains the technical limitations that govern the search to the case agent and prosecutor, creates the plan for executing the search, and in many cases takes the lead role in executing the search itself.

Finally, the prosecutor reviews the affidavit and warrant and makes sure that the entire process complies with the US Fourth Amendment and Rule 41 of the Federal Rules of Criminal Procedure. Of course, each member of the team should collaborate with the others to help ensure an effective search. There are many sources of technical expertise in the federal government. Most agencies that have law enforcement investigators also have technical specialists trained in computer forensics. For example, the FBI has Computer Analysis Response Team (CART) examiners, the Internal Revenue Service has Seized Computer Evidence Recovery (SCER) specialists, and the Secret Service has the Electronic Crime Special Agent Program (ESCAP). Investigating agents should contact the technical experts within their own agency. Further, some agencies offer case agents sufficient technical training that they may also be able to act as technical specialists. In such cases, the case agents normally do not need to consult with technical experts and can serve as technical specialists and case agents simultaneously.

b) Learn as much as possible about the computer system that will be searched before devising a search strategy or drafting the warrant. After assembling the team, the case agent should begin acquiring as much information as possible about the computer system targeted by the search. It is difficult to overstate the importance of this step. For the most part, the need for detailed and accurate information about the targeted computer results from practical considerations. Until the agent has learned what kinds of computers and operating systems the target uses, it is impossible to know how the information the system contains can be retrieved, or even where the information may be located. Every computer and computer network is different, and subtle differences in hardware, software, operating systems, and system configuration can alter the search plan dramatically. For example, a particular search strategy may work well if a targeted network runs the Linux operating system, but might not work if the network runs Windows NT instead. These concerns are particularly important when searches involve complicated computer networks (as opposed to stand-alone PCs). For example, the mere fact that a business uses computers in its offices does not mean that the computers' terminals found there actually contain any useful information. Businesses may contract with network service providers that store the business' s information on remote network servers located miles (or even thousands of miles) away. As a result of these considerations, a technical specialist cannot advise the case agent on the practical aspects of different search strategies without knowing the nature of the computer system to be searched. Agents need to learn as much as possible about the targeted computer before drafting the warrant, including (if possible) the hardware, the software, the operating system, and the configuration of the network. Obtaining detailed and accurate information about the targeted computer also has important legal implications. For example, the incidental seizure of First Amendment materials such as drafts of newsletters or web pages may implicate the Privacy Protection Act (' PPA'), 42 U.S.C. and the incidental seizure and subsequent search through network accounts may raise issues under the Electronic Communications Privacy Act (' ECPA'). To minimize liability under these statutes, agents should conduct a careful investigation into whether and where First Amendment materials and network accounts may be stored on the computer system targeted by the search. At least one court has suggested that a failure to conduct such an investigation can help deprive the government of a good faith defense against liability under these statutes. On a practical level, agents may take various approaches to learning about a targeted computer network. In some cases, agents can interview the system administrator of the targeted network (sometimes in an undercover capacity), and obtain all or most of the information the technical specialist needs to plan and execute the search. When this is impossible or dangerous, more piecemeal strategies may prove effective. For example, agents sometimes conduct on-site visits (often undercover) that at least reveal some elements of the hardware involved. A useful source of information for networks connected to the Internet is the Internet itself. For example, the 'host' command in a UNIX environment often reveals the operating system, machines, and general layout of a targeted network connected to the Internet.

c) Formulate a strategy for conducting the search (including a backup plan) based on the known information about the targeted computer system. With a team in place and the targeted system researched, the next step is to formulate a strategy for conducting the search. For example, will the agents search through the targeted computer(s) on the premises, or will they simply enter the premises and remove all of the hardware? Will the agents make copies of individual files, or will they make exact copies of entire hard drives? What will the agents do if their original plan fails, or if the computer hardware or software turns out to be significantly different from what they expected? These decisions hinge on a series of practical and legal considerations. In most cases, the search team should decide on a preferred search strategy, and then plan a series of backup strategies if the preferred strategy proves impractical.

d) Draft the warrant, taking special care to describe the object of the search and the property to be seized accurately and particularly, and explain the search strategy (as well as the practical and legal issues that helped shape it) in the supporting affidavit. In general, however, the keys to drafting successful computer search warrants are first to describe carefully and particularly the object of the warrant that investigators have probable cause to seize, and second to explain adequately the search strategy in the supporting affidavit. On a practical level, these steps help focus and guide the investigators as they execute the search. As a legal matter, the first step helps to overcome particularity challenges, and the latter helps to thwart claims that the agents executed the search in 'flagrant disregard' of the warrant.

Computer search strategies often depend on the role of the hardware in the offense. If the hardware is itself evidence, an instrumentality, contraband, or a fruit of crime, agents will usually plan to seize the hardware and search its contents off-site. If the hardware is merely a storage device for evidence, agents generally will only seize the hardware if less disruptive alternatives are not feasible. In general, computer hardware can serve one of two roles in a criminal case. First, the computer hardware can be a storage device for evidence of crime. For example, if a suspect keeps evidence of his fraud schemes stored in his personal computer, the hardware itself is merely a container for evidence. The purpose of searching the suspect' s computer will be to recover the evidence the computer hardware happens to contain. In other cases, however, computer hardware can itself be contraband, evidence, an instrumentality, or a fruit of crime. For example, a computer used to transmit child pornography is an instrumentality of crime, and stolen computers are contraband. In such cases, Federal Rule of Criminal Procedure 41 grants agents the right to seize the computer itself, independently from the materials that the hardware happens to contain. Because Rule 41 authorizes agents to seize hardware in the latter case but not the former, the search strategy for a particular computer search hinges first on the role of the hardware in the offense.

a) *When Hardware Is Itself Contraband, Evidence, or an Instrumentality or Fruit of Crime*: Under Fed. R. Crim. P. 41(b), agents may obtain search warrants to seize computer hardware if the hardware is contraband, evidence, or an instrumentality or fruit of crime. When the hardware itself may be seized according to Rule 41, agents will usually conduct the search by seizing the computer and searching it off-site. For example, a home personal computer used to store and transmit contraband images is itself an instrumentality of the crime. Accordingly, Rule 41 permits agents to obtain a warrant authorizing the seizure of the computer hardware. In most cases, investigators will simply obtain a warrant to seize the computer, seize the hardware during the search, and then search through the defendant' s computer for the contraband files back at the police station or computer forensics laboratory. In such cases, the agents should explain in the supporting affidavit that they plan to search the computer for evidence and/or contraband after the computer has been seized and removed from the site of the search. Notably, exceptions exist when agents will not want to seize computer hardware even when the hardware is used as an instrumentality, evidence, contraband, or a fruit of crime. When the 'computer' involved is not a stand-alone PC but rather part of a complicated network, the collateral damage and practical headaches that would arise from seizing the entire network generally counsels against a wholesale seizure. For example, if a system administrator of a computer network stores stolen proprietary information somewhere in the network, the network becomes an instrumentality of the system administrator' s crime. Technically, agents could obtain a warrant to seize the entire network. However, carting off the entire network might cripple a functioning business and disrupt the lives of hundreds of people, as well as subject the government to civil suits under the Privacy Protection Act and the Electronic Communications Privacy Act. In such circumstances, agents will want to take a more nuanced approach to obtain the evidence they need. Agents faced with such a situation can call the Computer Crime and Intellectual Property Section at (202) 514-1026 or the Assistant U.S. Attorney designated as a Computer-Telecommunications Coordinator (CTC) in their district for more specific advice.

b) *When Hardware is Merely a Storage Device for Evidence of Crime*: The strategy for conducting a computer search is significantly different if the computer hardware is merely a storage device for evidence of a crime. In such cases, Rule 41(b) authorizes agents to obtain a warrant to seize the electronic evidence, but arguably does not authorize the agents to seize the hardware that happens to contain that evidence. Cf. United States v. Tamura, 694 F.2d 591, 595 (noting that probable cause to seize specific paper files enumerated in warrant technically does permit the seizure of commingled innocent files). The hardware is merely a storage container for evidence, not evidence itself. This does not mean that the government cannot seize the equipment: rather, it means that the government generally should only seize the equipment if a less intrusive alternative that permits the effective recovery of the evidence is infeasible in the particular circumstances of the case. As a practical matter, circumstances will often require investigators to seize equipment and search its contents off-site. First, it may take days or weeks to find the specific information described in the warrant because computer storage devices can contain extraordinary amounts of information. Agents cannot reasonably be expected to spend more than a few hours searching for materials on-site, and in some circumstances (such as executing a search at a suspect' s home) even a few hours may be unreasonable. Given that personal computers sold in the year 2000 usually can store the equivalent of ten million pages of information and networks can store hundreds of times that (and these capacities double nearly every year), it may be practically impossible for agents to search quickly through a computer for specific data, a particular file, or a broad set of files while on-site. Even if the agents know specific information about the files they seek, the data may be mislabeled, encrypted, stored in hidden directories, or embedded in 'slack space' that a simple file listing will ignore. Recovering the evidence may require painstaking analysis by an expert in the controlled environment of a forensics laboratory.

Attempting to search files on-site may even risk damaging the evidence itself in some cases. Agents executing a search may learn on-site that the computer employs an uncommon operating system that the on-site technical specialist does not fully understand. Because an inartful attempt to conduct a search may destroy evidence, the best strategy may be to remove the hardware so that a government expert in that particular operating system can examine the computer later. Off-site searches also may be necessary if agents have reason to believe that the computer has been 'booby trapped' by a savvy criminal. Technically adept users may know how to trip-wire their computers with self-destruct programs that could erase vital evidence if the system were examined by anyone other than an expert. For example, a criminal could write a very short program that would cause the computer to demand a password periodically, and if the correct password is not entered within ten seconds, would trigger the automatic destruction of the computer' s files. In these cases, it is best to seize the equipment and permit an off-site expert to disarm the program before any search occurs. In light of these uncertainties, agents often plan to try to search on-site, with the understanding that they will seize the equipment if circumstances discovered on-site make an on-site search infeasible. Once on-site to execute the search, the agents will assess the hardware, software, and resources available to determine whether an on-site search is possible. In many cases, the search strategy will depend on the sensitivity of the environment in which the search occurs. For example, agents seeking to obtain information stored on the computer network of a functioning business will in most circumstances want to make every effort to obtain the information without seizing the business' s computers, if possible. In such situations, a tiered search strategy designed to use the least intrusive approach that will recover the information is generally appropriate. Whatever search strategy is chosen, it should be explained fully in the affidavit supporting the warrant application. Sometimes, conducting a search on-site will be possible. A friendly employee or system administrator may agree to pinpoint a file or record or may have a recent backup, permitting the agents to obtain a hard copy of the files they seek while on-site. Alternatively, agents may be able to locate the set of files targeted and make electronic copies, or may be able to mirror a segment of the storage drive based on knowledge that the information exists somewhere within that segment of the drive. In other cases, of course, such strategies will fail. If the agents cannot learn where the information is stored or cannot create a working mirror image for technical reasons, they may have no choice but to seize the computer and remove it. Because personal computers are easily moved and can be searched effectively off-site using special

> forensics tools, agents are particularly likely to seize personal computers absent unusual circumstances. The general strategy is to pursue the quickest, least intrusive, and most direct search strategy that is consistent with securing the evidence described in the warrant. This strategy will permit agents to search on-site in some cases, and will permit them to seize the computers for off-site review in others. Flexibility is the key.

Agents should obtain multiple warrants if they have reason to believe that a network search will retrieve data stored in multiple locations. Fed. R. Crim. states that

> a magistrate judge located in one judicial district may issue a search warrant for 'a search of property . . . within the district,' or 'a search of property . . . outside the district if the property . . . is within the district when the warrant is sought but might move outside the district before the warrant is executed.'

The Supreme Court has held that 'property' as described in Rule 41 includes intangible property such as computer data. Although the courts have not directly addressed the matter, the language of Rule 41 combined with the Supreme Court' s interpretation of 'property' may limit searches of computer data to data that resides in the district in which the warrant was issued.

A territorial limit on searches of computer data poses problems for law enforcement because computer data stored in a computer network can be located anywhere in the world. For example, agents searching an office in Manhattan pursuant to a warrant from the Southern District of New York may sit down at a terminal and access information stored remotely on a computer located in New Jersey, California, or even a foreign country. A single file described by the warrant could be located anywhere on the planet, or could be divided up into several locations in different districts or countries. Even worse, it may be impossible for agents to know when they execute their search whether the data they are seizing has been stored within the district or outside of the district. Agents may in some cases be able to learn where the data is located before the search, but in others they will be unable to know the storage site of the data until after the search has been completed.

When agents can learn prior to the search that some or all of the data described by the warrant is stored remotely from where the agents will execute the search, the best course of action depends upon where the remotely stored data is located. When the data is stored remotely in two or more different places within the United States and its territories, agents should obtain additional warrants for each location where the data resides to ensure compliance with a strict reading of Rule 41(a). For example, if the data is stored in two different districts, agents should obtain separate warrants from the two districts. Agents should also include a thorough explanation of the location of the data and the proposed means of conducting the search in the affidavits accompanying the warrants.

When agents learn before a search that some or all of the data is stored remotely outside of the United States, matters become more complicated. The United States may be required to take actions ranging from informal notice to a formal request for assistance to the country concerned.

Further, some countries may object to attempts by U.S. law enforcement to access computers located within their borders. Although the search may seem domestic to a U.S. law enforcement officer executing the search in the

United States pursuant to a valid warrant, other countries may view matters differently.

When agents do not and even cannot know that data searched from one district is actually located outside the district, evidence seized remotely from another district ordinarily should not lead to suppression of the evidence obtained. The reasons for this are twofold. First, courts may conclude that agents sitting in one district who search a computer in that district and unintentionally cause intangible information to be sent from a second district into the first have complied with US Rule 41(a). Second, even if courts conclude that the search violates Rule 41(a), the violation will not lead to suppression of the evidence unless the agents intentionally and deliberately disregarded the Rule, or the violation leads to 'prejudice' in the sense that the search might not have occurred or would not have been so 'abrasive' if the Rule had been followed. Under the widely-adopted Burke test, courts generally deny motions to suppress when agents executing the search cannot know whether it violates Rule 41 either legally or factually. Accordingly, evidence acquired from a network search that accessed data stored in multiple districts should not lead to suppression unless the agents intentionally and deliberately disregarded Rule 41(a) or prejudice resulted.

Agents must announce their presence and authority prior to executing a search warrant. This so-called 'knock and announce' rule reduces the risk of violence and destruction of property when agents execute a search. The rule is not absolute, however. In Richards v. Wisconsin, the Supreme Court held that agents can dispense with the knock-and-announce requirement if they have a reasonable suspicion that knocking and announcing their presence, under the particular circumstances, would be dangerous or futile, or that it would inhibit the effective investigation of the crime by, for example, allowing the destruction of evidence. The Court stated that this showing was 'not high, but the police should be required to make it whenever the reasonableness of a no-knock entry is challenged.' Such a showing satisfies both the Fourth Amendment and the statutory knock-and-announce rule of 18 U.S.C. ' Agents may need to conduct no-knock searches in computer crime cases because technically adept suspects may 'hot wire' their computers in an effort to destroy evidence.

For example, technically adept computer hackers have been known to use 'hot keys,' computer programs that destroy evidence when a special button is pressed. If agents knock at the door to announce their search, the suspect can simply press the button and activate the program to destroy the evidence.

When agents have reason to believe that knocking and announcing their presence would allow the destruction of evidence, would be dangerous, or would be futile, agents should request that the magistrate judge issue a no-knock warrant. The failure to obtain judicial authorization to dispense with the knock-and-announce rule does not preclude the agents from conducting a no-knock search, however. In some cases, agents may neglect to request a no-knock warrant, or may not have reasonable suspicion that evidence will be destroyed until they execute the search. In Richards, the Supreme Court made clear that 'the reasonableness of the officers' decision [to dispense with the knock-and-announce rule] . . . must be evaluated as of the time they entered' the area to be searched.

Accordingly, agents may 'exercise independent judgment' and decide to conduct a no-knock search when they execute the search, even if they did not request such authority or the magistrate judge specifically refused to authorize a no-knock search. The question in all such cases is whether the agents had 'a reasonable suspicion that knocking and announcing their presence, under the particular circumstances, would be dangerous or futile, or that it would inhibit the effective investigation of the crime by, for example, allowing the destruction of evidence.'

Despite Rule 41(d), courts have authorized 'sneak-and-peek' warrants in a few narrow situations. Sometimes called 'surreptitious search warrants,' sneak-and-peek warrants are warrants that excuse agents from having to notify the person whose premises are searched that the search has occurred at the time of the search. Because notice furthers important constitutional values, it is important that agents who wish to obtain sneak-and-peek warrants should do so sparingly, and only in special circumstances. However, sneak-and-peek searches may prove useful in searches for intangible computer data. For example, agents executing a sneak-and-peek warrant to search a computer may be able to enter a business after hours, search the computer, and then exit the business without leaving any sign that the search occurred.

The circuits that have considered the legality of sneak-and-peek warrants have struggled to reconcile them with Rule 41(d) and the Fourth Amendment. The Second and Ninth Circuits each set forth two requirements that must be met in the absence of explicit statutory authority before a sneak-and-peek warrant may be authorized. First, the officers must make a showing of 'reasonable necessity' as to why the officers should be able to delay notice of the search.

Second, the warrant must require notice to the target of the search within seven days of the surreptitious search unless a 'strong showing of necessity' for further delay has been made. Although other circuits may take a less restrictive approach, these two requirements provide a useful standard that agents should follow when they seek judicial authorization to conduct a sneak-and-peek search.

If these two requirements are met, a court will permit evidence obtained in violation of Rule 41 to be used in court so long as 1) the covert nature of the search did not prejudice the target, in the sense that the search might not have occurred if notice had been given, and 2) the agents did not intentionally and deliberately disregard Rule 41 in executing the search. Agents executing a sneak-and-peek search will not be deemed to have intentionally and deliberately disregarded Rule 41 if the warrant authorized the sneak-and-peek search, or the executing agents believed that the warrant authorized such a search. Finally, a showing of good faith reliance on a sneak-and-peek warrant will defeat a suppression motion.

Agents must exercise special care when planning a computer search that may result in the seizure of legally privileged documents such as medical records or attorney-client communications. Two issues must be considered. First, agents should make sure that the search will not violate the Attorney General' s regulations relating to obtaining confidential information from disinterested third parties. Second, agents should devise a strategy for reviewing the seized computer files following the search so that no breach of a privilege occurs.

a) *The Attorney General' s Regulations Relating to Searches of Disinterested Lawyers, Physicians, and Clergymen*: Agents should be very careful if they plan to search the office of a doctor, lawyer, or member of the clergy who is not implicated in the crime under investigation. At Congress' s direction, the Attorney General has issued guidelines for federal officers who want to obtain documentary materials from such disinterested third parties. Under these rules, federal law enforcement officers should not use a search warrant to obtain documentary materials believed to be in the private possession of a disinterested third party physician, lawyer, or clergyman where the material sought or likely to be reviewed during the execution of the warrant contains confidential information on patients, clients, or parishioners. The regulation does contain a narrow exception. A search warrant can be used if using less intrusive means would substantially jeopardize the availability or usefulness of the materials sought; access to the documentary materials appears to be of substantial importance to the investigation; and the application for the warrant has been recommended by the U.S. Attorney and approved by the appropriate Deputy Assistant Attorney General. When planning to search the offices of a lawyer under investigation, agents should follow the guidelines offered in the United States Attorney' s Manual, and should consult the Office of Enforcement Operations.

b) *Strategies for Reviewing Privileged Computer Files*: Agents contemplating a search that may result in the seizure of legally privileged computer files should devise a post-seizure strategy for screening out the privileged files and should describe that strategy in the affidavit. When agents seize a computer that contains legally privileged files, a trustworthy third party must comb through the files to separate those files within the scope of the warrant from files that contain privileged material. After reviewing the files, the third party will offer those files within the scope of the warrant to the prosecution team. Preferred practices for determining who will comb through the files vary widely among different courts. In general, however, there are three options. First, the court itself may review the files in camera. Second, the presiding judge may appoint a neutral third party known as a 'special master' to the task of reviewing the files. Third, a team of prosecutors who are not working on the case may form a 'taint team' or 'privilege team' to help execute the search and review the files afterwards. The taint team sets up a so-called 'Chinese Wall' between the evidence and the prosecution team, permitting only unprivileged files that are within the scope of the warrant to slip through the wall. Because a single computer can store millions of files, judges will undertake in camera review of computer files only rarely. Instead, the typical choice is between using a taint team and a special master. Most prosecutors will prefer to use a taint team if the court consents. A taint team can usually screen through the seized computer files fairly quickly, whereas special masters often take several years to complete their review. Although no single standard has emerged, these courts have generally indicated that evidence screened by a taint team will be admissible only if the government shows that its procedures adequately protected the defendants' rights and no prejudice occurred. In unusual circumstances, the court may conclude that a taint team would be inadequate and may appoint a special master to review the files. In any event, the reviewing authority will almost certainly need a skilled and neutral technical expert to assist in sorting, identifying, and analyzing digital evidence for the reviewing process.

c) *Drafting the Warrant and Affidavit*: Law enforcement officers must draft two documents to obtain a search warrant from a magistrate judge. The first document is the affidavit, a sworn statement that (at a minimum) explains the basis for the affiant' s belief that the search is justified by probable cause. The second document is the proposed warrant itself. The proposed warrant typically is a one-page form, plus attachments incorporated by reference, that describes the place to be searched, and the persons or things to be seized. If the magistrate judge agrees that the affidavit establishes probable cause, and that the proposed warrant' s descriptions of the place to be searched and things to be seized are adequately particular, the magistrate judge will sign the warrant. Under the Federal Rules of Criminal Procedure, officers must execute the warrant within ten days after the warrant has been signed.

Agents must take special care when describing the computer files or hardware to be seized, either in the warrant itself or (more likely) in an attachment to the warrant incorporated into the warrant by reference. The Fourth Amendment requires that every warrant must particularly describe the things to be seized.

The particularity requirement prevents law enforcement from executing 'general warrants' that permit 'exploratory rummaging' through a person' s belongings in search of evidence of a crime. The particularity requirement has two distinct elements. First, the warrant must describe the things to be seized with sufficiently precise language so that it tells the officers how to separate the items properly subject to seizure from irrelevant items. Second, the description of the things to be seized must not be so broad that it encompasses items that should not be seized. Put another way, the description in the warrant of the things to be seized should be limited to the scope of the probable cause established in the warrant. Considered together, the elements forbid agents from obtaining 'general warrants' and instead require agents to conduct narrow seizures that attempt to 'minimize unwarranted intrusions upon privacy.'

If computer hardware is contraband, evidence, fruits, or instrumentalities of crime, the warrant should describe the hardware itself. If the probable cause relates only to information, however, the warrant should describe the information, rather than the physical storage devices which happen to contain it. The most important decision agents must make when describing the property in the warrant is whether the seizable property according to Rule 41 is the computer hardware itself, or merely the information that the hardware contains. If the computer hardware is itself contraband, an instrumentality of crime, or evidence, the focus of the warrant should be on the computer hardware itself and not on the information it contains. The warrant should describe the hardware and indicate that the hardware will be seized. However, if the probable cause relates only to information stored on the computer, the warrant should focus on the content of the relevant files rather than on the storage devices which may happen to contain them. The warrant should describe the information based on its content (e.g., gambling records, evidence of a fraud scheme), and then request the authority to seize the information in whatever form the information may be stored.

When conducting a search for information, agents need to consider carefully exactly what information they need. The information may be very narrow (e.g., a specific record or report), or quite broad (e.g., thousands of records relating to an elaborate fraud scheme). Agents should tailor each warrant to the needs of each search. The warrant should describe the information to be seized, and then request the authority to seize the information in whatever form it may be stored (whether electronic or not). Agents should be particularly careful when seeking authority to seize a broad class of information. This often occurs when agents plan to search computers at a business. Agents cannot simply request permission to seize 'all records' from an operating business unless agents have probable cause to believe that the criminal activity under investigation pervades the entire business. Instead, the description of the files to be seized should include limiting phrases that can modify and limit the 'all records' search. For example, agents may specify the crime under investigation, the target of the investigation if known, and the time frame of the records involved.

Agents should narrow 'all records' searches with limiting language where necessary and appropriate. One effective approach is to begin with an 'all records' description; add limiting language stating the crime, the suspects, and relevant time period if applicable; include explicit examples of the records to be seized; and then indicate that the records may be seized in any form, whether electronic or non-electronic. For example, when drafting a warrant to search a computer at a business for evidence of a drug trafficking crime, agents might describe the property to be seized in the following way:

All records relating to violations of drug trafficking and conspiracy to traffic drugs involving [the suspect] since January 1, 1996, including lists of customers and related identifying information; types, amounts, and prices of drugs trafficked as well as dates, places, and amounts of specific transactions; any information related to sources of narcotic drugs (including names, addresses, phone numbers, or any other identifying information); any information recording [the suspect' s] schedule or travel from 1995 to the present; all bank records, checks, credit card bills, account information, and other financial records.

The terms 'records' and 'information' include all of the foregoing items of evidence in whatever form and by whatever means they may have been created or stored, including any electrical, electronic, or magnetic form (such as any information on an electronic or magnetic storage device, including floppy diskettes, hard disks, ZIP disks, CD-ROMs, optical discs, backup tapes, printer buffers, smart cards, memory calculators, pagers, personal digital assistants such as Palm Pilot computers, as well as printouts or readouts from any magnetic storage device); any handmade form (such as writing, drawing, painting); any mechanical form (such as printing or typing); and any photographic form (such as microfilm, microfiche, prints, slides, negatives, videotapes, motion pictures, photocopies). This language describes the general class of information to be seized ('

all records'); narrows it to the extent possible (only those records involving the defendant' s drug trafficking activities since 1995); offers examples of the types of records sought (such as customer lists and bank records); and then explains the various forms that the records may take (including electronic and non-electronic forms). Of course, agents do not need to follow this approach in every case; judicial review of search warrants is 'commonsensical' and 'practical,' rather than 'overly technical.' United States v. Ventresca. When agents cannot know the precise form that records will take before the search occurs, a generic description must suffice.

Search warrants may be subject to challenge when the description of the 'things to be seized' does not comply fully with the best practices described above. Two challenges to the scope of warrants arise particularly often. First, defendants may claim that a warrant is insufficiently particular when the warrant authorizes the seizure of hardware but the affidavit only establishes probable cause to seize information. Second, defendants may claim that agents exceeded the scope of the warrant by seizing computer equipment if the warrant failed to state explicitly that the information to be seized might be in electronic form. The former challenge argues that the description of the property to be seized was too broad, and the latter argues that the description was not broad enough.

1) *When the warrant authorizes the seizure of hardware but the affidavit only establishes probable cause to seize information*: Computer search warrants sometimes authorize the seizure of hardware when the probable cause in the affidavit relates solely to the computer files the hardware contains. For example, agents may

have probable cause to believe that a suspect possesses evidence of a fraud scheme, and may draft the warrant to authorize the seizure of the defendant' s computer equipment rather than the data stored within it. On a practical level, such a description makes sense because it accurately and precisely describes what the agents will do when they execute the warrant (i.e., seize the computer equipment). From a legal standpoint, however, the description is less than ideal: the equipment itself is not evidence of a crime, an instrumentality or contraband that may be seized according to Rule 41(a). The physical equipment merely stores the information that the agents have probable cause to seize. Although the agents may need to seize the equipment in order to obtain the files it contains, the better practice is to describe the information rather than the equipment in the warrant itself. When agents obtain a warrant authorizing the seizure of equipment, defendants may claim that the description of the property to be seized is fatally overbroad. To date, the courts have adopted a forgiving stance when faced with this challenge. The courts have generally held that descriptions of hardware can satisfy the particularity requirement so long as the subsequent searches of the seized computer hardware appear reasonably likely to yield evidence of crime. Despite these decisions, agents should comply with the technical requirements of Rule 41 when describing the 'property to be seized' in a search warrant. If the property to be seized is information, the warrant should describe the information to be seized, rather than its container. Of course, when the information to be seized is contraband (such as child pornography), the container itself may be independently seized as an instrumentality.

2) *When agents seize computer data and computer hardware but the warrant does not expressly authorize their seizure*: Search warrants sometimes fail to mention that information described in the warrant may appear in electronic form. For example, a search for 'all records' relating to a conspiracy may list paper-world examples of record documents but neglect to state that the records may be stored within a computer. Agents executing the search who come across computer equipment may not know whether the warrant authorizes the seizure of the computers. If the agents do seize the computers, defense counsel may file a motion to suppress the evidence arguing that the computers seized were beyond the scope of the warrant. The courts have generally permitted agents to seize computer equipment when agents reasonably believe that the content described in the warrant may be stored there, regardless of whether the warrant states expressly that the information may be stored in electronic form. As the Tenth Circuit explained in United States v. Reyes, 'in the age of modern technology and commercial availability of various forms of items, the warrant c[an] not be expected to describe with exactitude the precise form the records would take.'

3) *General defenses to challenges of computer search warrants based on the description of the 'things to be seized*: Prosecutors facing challenges to the particularity of computer search warrants have a number of additional arguments that may save inartfully drawn warrants. First, prosecutors can argue that the agents

who executed the search had an objectively reasonable good faith belief that the warrant was sufficiently particular. If true, the court will not order suppression of the evidence. Second, prosecutors may argue that the broad description in the warrant must be read in conjunction with a more particular description contained in the supporting affidavit. Finally, several circuits have held that courts can redact overbroad language and admit evidence from overbroad seizures if the evidence admitted was seized pursuant to sufficiently particular language.

The second step in preparing a warrant to search and seize a computer is to write a sworn affidavit establishing probable cause to believe that contraband, evidence, fruits, or instrumentalities of crime exist in the location to be searched. According to the Supreme Court, the affidavit must establish 'a fair probability that contraband or evidence of a crime will be found in a particular place.' This requires a practical, common-sense determination of the probabilities, based on a totality of the circumstances. Of course, probable cause will not exist if the agent can only point to a 'bare suspicion' that criminal evidence will be found in the place searched. Once a magistrate judge finds probable cause and issues the warrant, the magistrate' s determination that probable cause existed is entitled to 'great deference,' Gates, and will be upheld so long as there is a 'substantial basis for concluding that probable cause existed.'

The probable cause requirement does not require agents to be clairvoyant in their knowledge of the precise forms of evidence or contraband that will exist in the location to be searched. For example, agents do not need probable cause to believe that the evidence sought will be found in computerized form. Similarly, agents do not need to know exactly what statutory violation the evidence will help reveal. Prandy-Binett, and do not need to know who owns the property to be searched and seized. The probable cause standard simply requires agents to establish a fair probability that contraband or evidence of a crime will be found in the particular place to be searched. Of course, agents who have particular knowledge as to the form of evidence or contraband that exists at the place to be searched should articulate that knowledge fully in the affidavit. Probable cause challenges to computer search warrants arise particularly often in cases involving the possession and transmission of child pornography images.

For example, defendants often claim that the passage of time between the warrant application and the occurrence of the incriminating facts alleged in the affidavit left the magistrate judge without sufficient reason to believe that images of child pornography would be found in the defendant' s computers. The courts have generally found little merit in these 'staleness' arguments, in part because the courts have taken judicial notice of the fact that collectors of child pornography rarely dispose of such material. Probable cause challenges may also arise when supporting evidence in an affidavit derives heavily from records of a particular Internet account or Internet Protocol (' IP') address. The problem is a practical one: generally speaking, the fact that an account or address was used does not establish conclusively the identity or location of the particular person who used it. As a result, an affidavit based heavily on account or IP address logs must demonstrate a sufficient connection between the logs and the location to be searched to establish 'a fair probability that contraband or evidence of a crime will be found in [the] particular place' to be searched. In the Affidavit Supporting the Warrant, Include an Explanation of the Search Strategy (Such as the Need to Conduct an Off-site Search) as Well as the Practical and Legal Considerations That Will Govern the Execution of the Search

The third step in drafting a successful computer search warrant is to explain both the search strategy and the practical considerations underlying the strategy in the affidavit. For example, if agents expect that they may need to seize a personal computer and search it off-site to recover the relevant evidence, the affidavit should explain this expectation and its basis to the magistrate judge. The affidavit should inform the court of the practical limitations of conducting an on-site search, and should articulate the plan to remove the entire computer from the site if it becomes necessary.

The affidavit should also explain what techniques the agents expect to use to search the computer for the specific files that represent evidence of crime and may be intermingled with entirely innocuous documents. If the search strategy has been influenced by legal considerations such as potential PPA liability, the affidavit should explain how and why in the affidavit. If the agents have authority to seize hardware because the hardware itself is evidence, contraband, or an instrumentality of crime, the affidavit should explain whether the agents intend to search the hardware following the seizure, and, if so, for what.

In sum, the affidavit should address all of the relevant practical and legal issues that the agents have considered in the course of planning the search, and should explain the course of conduct that the agents will follow as a result. Finally, when the search strategy is complicated or the affidavit is under seal, it is a good practice for agents to reproduce the explanation of the search strategy contained in the affidavit as an attachment to the warrant itself. The reasons for articulating the search strategy in the affidavit are both practical and legal. On a practical level, explaining the search strategy in the affidavit creates a document that both the court and the agents can read and refer to as a guide to the execution of the search. Similarly, if the explanation of the search strategy is reproduced as an attachment to the warrant and given to the subject of the search pursuant to Rule 41(d), the explanation permits the owner of the searched property to satisfy himself during the search that the agents' conduct is within the scope of the warrant. Finally, as a legal matter, explaining the search strategy in the affidavit helps to counter defense counsel motions to suppress based on the agents' alleged 'flagrant disregard' of the warrant during the execution of the search. To understand motions to suppress based on the 'flagrant disregard' standard, agents and prosecutors should recall the limitations on search and seizure imposed by Rule 41 and the Fourth Amendment.

The US Fourth Amendment and Rule 41 limit agents to searching for and seizing property described in the warrant that is itself evidence, contraband, fruits, or instrumentalities of crime. If agents execute a warrant and seize additional property not described in the warrant, defense counsel can file a motion to suppress the additional evidence. Motions to suppress such additional evidence are filed relatively rarely because, if granted, they result only in the suppression of the property not named in the warrant. On the other hand, defense counsel will often attempt to use the seizure of additional property as the basis for a motion to suppress all of the evidence obtained in a search. To be entitled to the extreme remedy of blanket suppression, the defendant must establish that the seizure of additional materials proves that the agents executed the warrant in 'flagrant disregard' of its terms. A search is executed in 'flagrant disregard' of its terms when the officers so grossly exceed the scope of the warrant during execution that the authorized search appears to be merely a pretext for a 'fishing expedition' through the target' s private property.

Motions to suppress alleging 'flagrant disregard' are common in computer searches because, for practical and technical reasons, agents executing computer searches frequently must seize hardware or files that are not described in the warrant. For example, agents who have probable cause to believe that evidence of a defendant' s fraud scheme is stored on the defendant' s home computer may have to seize the entire computer and search it off-site.

Defense lawyers often argue that by seizing more than the specific computer files named in the warrant, the agents 'flagrantly disregarded' the seizure authority granted by the warrant. Prosecutors can best respond to 'flagrant disregard' motions by showing that any seizure of property not named in the warrant resulted from a good faith response to inherent practical difficulties, rather than a wish to conduct a general search of the defendant' s property under the guise of a narrow warrant. The courts have recognized the practical difficulties that agents face in conducting computer searches for specific files, and have approved off-site searches despite the incidental seizure of additional property.

The decisions permitting off-site computer searches are bolstered by analogous 'physical-world' cases that have authorized agents to remove file cabinets and boxes of paper documents so that agents can review the contents off-site for the documents named in the warrant. Explaining the agent' s search strategy and the practical considerations underlying the strategy in the affidavit can help ensure that the execution of the search will not be deemed in 'flagrant disregard' of the warrant. A careful explanation of the search strategy illustrates the agent' s good faith and due care, articulates the practical concerns driving the search, and permits the judge to authorize the strategy described in the affidavit. A search that complies with the strategy explained in the supporting affidavit will not be in flagrant disregard of the warrant. When agents expect that the files described in the warrant will be commingled with innocent files outside of the warrant' s scope, it is a good practice, if technically possible, to explain in the affidavit how the agents plan to search the computer for the targeted files.

When agents conduct a search for computer files and other electronic evidence stored in a hard drive or other storage device, the evidence may be commingled with data and files that have no relation to the crime under investigation. Figuring out how best to locate and retrieve the evidence amidst the unrelated data is more of an art than a science, and often requires significant technical expertise and careful attention to the facts. As a result, agents may or may not know at the time the warrant is obtained how the storage device should be searched, and, in beginning the search, may or may not know whether it will be possible to locate the evidence without conducting an extensive search through unrelated files.

When agents have a factual basis for believing that they can locate the evidence using a specific set of techniques, the affidavit should explain the techniques that the agents plan to use to distinguish incriminating documents from commingled documents. Depending on the circumstances, it may be helpful to consult with experts in computer forensics to determine what kind of search can be conducted to locate the particular files described in the warrant. In some cases, a 'key word' search or similar surgical approach may be possible. Such an approach may permit law enforcement to locate the incriminating files without conducting an extensive search through innocent files that happen to be mixed together with the incriminating files that are the target of the search. Notably, the Fourth Amendment does not generally require such an approach. Of course, in many cases a narrow approach will be technically impossible. The targeted files may be mislabeled, hidden, oddly configured, written using code words to escape detection, encrypted, or otherwise impossible to find using a simple technique such as a 'key word' search.

Because some judges may fail to appreciate such technical difficulties, it is a good practice as a matter of policy for agents to discuss these issues in the affidavit if it appears that a narrow search will not be effective. In such cases, a more extensive search through innocent files will be necessary to determine which files fall within the scope of the warrant. Explaining these practical needs in the affidavit can make clear at the outset why an extensive search will not be in 'flagrant disregard' of the warrant, and why the extensive search complies fully with traditional Fourth Amendment principles.

When agents obtain a warrant to seize hardware that is itself evidence, contraband, or an instrumentality of crime, they should explain in the affidavit whether and how they plan to search the hardware following the seizure. When agents have probable cause to seize hardware because it is evidence, contraband, or an instrumentality of crime, the warrant will ordinarily describe the property to be seized as the hardware itself. In many of these cases, however, the agents will plan to search the hardware after it is seized for electronic data stored inside the hardware that also constitute evidence or contraband. It is a good practice for agents to inform the magistrate of this plan in the supporting affidavit. Although the courts have upheld searches when agents did not explain this expectation in the affidavit.

In many cases, computer equipment that has been seized will be sent to a laboratory for forensic examination. The time that may elapse before a technical specialist completes the forensic examination varies widely, depending on the hardware itself, the evidence sought, and the urgency of the search. In most cases, however, the elapsed time is a matter of months. Several legal issues may arise during the post-seizure period that implicate the government' s right to retain and search the computers in their custody.

Agents should obtain a second warrant to search a computer seized pursuant to a valid warrant if the property targeted by the proposed search is different from that underlying the first warrant. Agents often seize a computer pursuant to a warrant, and then ask whether they need a second warrant to search the computer.

Whether a second warrant is needed depends on the purpose of the search. If agents plan to search the computer for the information that was the target of the original seizure, no second warrant is required.

For example, in United States v. Simpson, investigators obtained a warrant to seize the defendant' s 'computer diskettes . . . and the defendant' s computer' based on probable cause to believe it contained child pornography. The investigators seized the computer and then searched it in police custody, finding child pornography images. On appeal following conviction, the defendant claimed that the investigators lacked the authority to search the computer because the warrant merely authorized the seizure of equipment. The Tenth Circuit rejected the argument, concluding that a warrant to seize computer equipment permitted agents to search the equipment. If investigators seize computer equipment for the evidence it contains and later decide to search the equipment for different evidence, however, they should obtain a second warrant. In United States v. Carey, detectives obtained a warrant to search the defendant' s computer for records of narcotics sales. Searching the computer back at the police station, a detective discovered images of child pornography. At that point, the detective 'abandoned the search for drug-related evidence' and instead searched the entire hard drive for evidence of child pornography. The Tenth Circuit suppressed the child pornography, holding that the subsequent search for child pornography was 'impermissible general rummaging' that exceeded the scope of the original warrant.

The US Supreme Court' s recent Fourth Amendment cases generally have declined to examine an agent' s subjective intent, and instead have focused on whether the circumstances, viewed objectively, justified the agent' s conduct. Neither Rule 41 nor the Fourth Amendment creates any specific time limits on the government' s forensic examination of seized computers. Some magistrate judges have begun imposing such limitations, however. Despite the best efforts of the government to analyze seized computers quickly, the forensic examination of seized computers often takes months to complete because computers can store enormous amounts of data. As a result, suspects whose computers have been seized may be deprived of their computer hardware for an extended period of time. Neither Rule 41 nor the Fourth Amendment imposes any specific limitation on the time period of the government' s forensic examination. The government ordinarily may retain the seized computer and examine its contents in a careful and deliberate manner without legal restrictions, subject only to Rule 41(e)' s authorization that a 'person aggrieved' by the seizure of property may bring a motion for the return of the property.

A few magistrate judges have taken a different view, however. Several magistrate judges have refused to sign search warrants authorizing the seizure of computers unless the government conducts the forensic examination in a short period of time, such as thirty days. Some magistrate judges have imposed time limits as short as seven days, and several have imposed specific time limits when agents apply for a warrant to seize computers from operating businesses. In support of these limitations, a few magistrate judges have expressed their concern that it might be constitutionally 'unreasonable' under the Fourth Amendment for the government to deprive individuals of their computers for more than a short period of time. Other magistrates have suggested that Rule 41' s requirement that agents execute a 'search' within 10 days of obtaining the warrant might apply to the forensic analysis of the computer as well as the initial search and seizure. The law does not expressly authorize magistrate judges to issue warrants that impose time limits on law enforcement' s examination of seized evidence.

Although the relevant case law is sparse, it suggests that magistrate judges lack the legal authority to refuse to issue search warrants on the ground that they believe that the agents may, in the future, execute the warrants in an unconstitutional fashion. In re Worksite Inspection of Quality Products, As the Supreme Court suggested in one early case, the proper course is for the magistrate to issue the warrant so long as probable cause exists, and then to permit the parties to litigate the constitutional issues afterwards. The refusal of the trial court to issue a warrant is in reality and effect, a refusal to permit the case to come to a hearing upon either questions of law or fact, and falls a little short of a refusal to permit the enforcement of the law.

Prosecutors should also be prepared to explain to magistrate judges why a forensic search for files stored in a seized computer need not occur within 10 days of obtaining the warrant. Rule 41(c)(1) requires that the agents who obtain a warrant must 'search, within a specified period of time not to exceed 10 days, the person or place named for the property or person specified.' This rule directs agents to search the place named in the warrant and seize the property specified within 10 days so that the warrant does not become 'stale' before it is executed. This rule does not apply to the forensic analysis of evidence that has already been seized, however; even if such analysis involves a Fourth Amendment 'search' in some cases, it plainly does not occur in 'the place . . . named' in the warrant. A Rule 41 warrant that authorizes the seizure of a book requires that the book must be seized from the place described in the warrant within 10 days.

However, neither the warrant nor Rule 41 requires law enforcement to examine the book and complete any forensic analysis of its pages within the same 10-day period. Although the legal basis for imposing time limits on forensic analysis is unclear, a magistrate judge' s refusal to issue a computer search warrant absent time limitations can create significant headaches for prosecutors. As a practical matter, prosecutors often have little choice but to go along with the magistrate judge' s wishes. A judge' s refusal to sign a search warrant generally is not an appealable final order, and the prosecutor' s only recourse is to turn to another judge, who will want to know why the first judge refused to sign the warrant. As a practical matter, then, prosecutors will often have little choice but to try to convince the judge not to impose a time limit, and if that fails, to request extensions when the time period proves impossible to follow.

At least one court has adopted the severe position that suppression is appropriate when the government fails to comply with court-imposed limits on the time period for reviewing seized computers. In United States v. Brunette, a magistrate judge permitted agents to seize the computers of a child pornography suspect on the condition that the agents searched through the computers for evidence 'within 30 days.' The agents executed the search five days later, and seized several computers.

A few days before the thirty-day period elapsed, the government applied for and obtained a thirty-day extension of the time for review. The agents then reviewed all but one of the seized computers within the thirty-day extension period, and found hundreds of images of child pornography.

However, the agents did not begin reviewing the last of the computers until two days after the extension period had elapsed. The defendant moved for suppression of the child pornography images found in the last computer, on the ground that the search outside of the sixty-day period violated the terms of the warrant and subsequent extension order. The court agreed, stating that

> 'because the Government failed to adhere to the requirements of the search warrant and subsequent order, any evidence gathered from the . . . computer is suppressed.'

The result in Brunette makes little sense either under Rule 41 or the Fourth Amendment. Even assuming that a magistrate judge has the authority to impose time constraints on forensic testing in the first place, it seems incongruous to impose suppression for violations of such conditions when analogous violations of Rule 41 itself would not result in suppression. CompareBrunettewith United States v. Twenty-Two Thousand, Two Hundred Eighty Seven Dollars, U.S. Currency, rejecting suppression when agents began search 'shortly after' 10 p.m., even though Rule 41 states that all searches must be conducted between 6:00 a.m. and 10 p.m.

This is especially true when the hardware to be searched was a container of contraband child pornography, and therefore was itself an instrumentality of crime that was not subject to return. Rule 41(e) Motions for Return of Property Rule 41(e) states:

> A person aggrieved by an unlawful search and seizure or by the deprivation of property may move the district court for the district in which the property was seized for the return of the property on the ground that such person is entitled to lawful possession of the property. The court shall receive evidence on any issue of fact necessary to the decision of the motion. If the motion is granted, the property shall be returned to the movant, although reasonable conditions may be imposed to protect access and use of the property in subsequent proceedings. If a motion for return of property is made or comes on for hearing in the district of trial after an indictment or information is filed, it shall be treated also as a motion to suppress under Rule 12.

Rule 41(e) has particular importance in computer search cases because it permits owners of seized computer equipment to move for the return of the equipment before an indictment is filed. In some cases, defendants will file such motions because they believe that the seizure of their equipment violated the Fourth Amendment. If they are correct, the equipment must be returned. Rule 41(e) also permits owners to move for a return of their property when the seizure was lawful, but the movant is 'aggrieved by the government' s continued possession of the seized property.'

The multi-functionality of computer equipment occasionally leads to Rule 41(e) motions on this basis. For example, a suspect under investigation for computer hacking may file a motion claiming that he must have his computer back to calculate his taxes or check his e-mail.

Similarly, a business suspected of fraud may file a motion for the return of its equipment claiming that it needs the equipment returned or else the business will suffer. Owners of properly seized computer equipment must overcome several formidable barriers before a court will order the government to return the equipment. First, the owner must convince the court that it should exercise equitable jurisdiction over the owner' s claim.

Although the jurisdictional standards vary widely among different courts, most courts will assert jurisdiction over a Rule 41(e) motion only if the movant establishes:

1) that being deprived of possession of the property causes 'irreparable injury' , and

2) that the movant is otherwise without a remedy at law.

If the United States has a need for the property in an investigation or prosecution, its retention of the property generally is reasonable. But, if the United States' legitimate interests can be satisfied even if the property is returned, continued retention of the property would be unreasonable. Rule 41(e) motions requesting the return of properly seized computer equipment succeed only rarely. First, courts will usually decline to exercise jurisdiction over the motion if the government has offered the property owner an electronic copy of the seized computer files. Second, courts that reach the merits generally find that the government' s interest in the computer equipment outweighs the defendant' s so long as a criminal prosecution or forfeiture proceeding is in the works. In the Matter of Search Warrant for K-Sports Imports, Inc., 163 F.R.D. 594, 597(denying motion for return of computer records relating to pending forfeiture proceedings). If the government does not plan to use the computers in further proceedings, however, the computer equipment must be returned. Further, a court may grant a Rule 41(e) motion if the defendant cannot operate his business without the seized computer equipment and the government can work equally well from a copy of the seized files.

The Fourth Amendment limits the ability of government agents to search for evidence without a warrant. It states:

> The right of the people to be secure in their persons, houses, papers, and effects, against unreasonable searches and seizures, shall not be violated, and no Warrants shall issue, but upon probable cause, supported by Oath or affirmation, and particularly describing the place to be searched, and the persons or things to be seized.

According to the Supreme Court, a warrantless search does not violate the Fourth Amendment if one of two conditions is satisfied. First, if the government' s conduct does not violate a person' s 'reasonable expectation of privacy,' then formally it does not constitute a Fourth Amendment 'search' and no warrant is required. Second, a warrantless search that violates a person' s reasonable expectation of privacy will nonetheless be 'reasonable' (and therefore constitutional) if it falls within an established exception to the warrant requirement. Accordingly, investigators must consider two issues when asking whether a government search of a computer requires a warrant. First, does the search violate a reasonable expectation of privacy? And if so, is the search nonetheless reasonable because it falls within an exception to the warrant requirement?

The Information Technology Act, 2000

The following Act of Parliament received the assent of the President on the 9th of June, 2000, and is hereby published for general information:

THE INFORMATION TECHNOLOGY ACT, 2000
(No. 21 of 2000) [9th June, 2000]

An Act to provide legal recognition for transactions carried out by means of electronic data interchange and other means of electronic communication, commonly referred to as "electronic commerce", which involve the use of alternatives to paper-based methods of communication and storage of information, to facilitate electronic filing of documents with the Government agencies and further to amend the Indian Penal Code, the Indian Evidence Act, 1872, the Bankers' Books Evidence Act, 1891 and the Reserve Bank of India Act, 1934 and for matters connected therewith or incidental thereto:

whereas the General Assembly of the United Nations by resolution A/RES/51/162, dated the 30th January, 1997 has adopted the Model Law on Electronic Commerce adopted by the United Nations Commission on International Trade Law;

and whereas the said resolution recommends *inter alia* that all States give favourable consideration to the said Model Law when they enact or revise their laws, in view of the need for uniformity of the law applicable to alternatives to paper-cased methods of communication and storage of information;

and whereas it is considered necessary to give effect to the said resolution and to promote efficient delivery of Government services by means of reliable electronic records.

be it enacted by Parliament in the Fifty-first Year of the Republic of India as follows:

CHAPTER I

PRELIMINARY

1. Short title, extent, commencement and application

1) This Act may be called the Information Technology Act, 2000.

2) It shall extend to the whole of India and, save as otherwise provided in this Act, it applies also to any offence or contravention thereunder committed outside India by any person.

3) It shall come into force on such date as the Central Government may, by notification, appoint and different dates may be appointed for different

provisions of this Act and any reference in any such provision to the commencement of this Act shall be construed as a reference to the commencement of that provision.

4) Nothing in this Act shall apply to:

   a) a negotiable instrument as defined in section 13 of the Negotiable Instruments Act, 1881;

   b) a power-of-attorney as defined in section 1A of the Powers-of-Attorney Act, 1882;

   c) a trust as defined in section 3 of the Indian Trusts Act, 1882;

   d) a will as defined in clause (h) of section 2 of the Indian Succession Act, 1925 including any other testamentary disposition by whatever name called;

   e) any contract for the sale or conveyance of immovable property or any interest in such property;

   f) any such class of documents or transactions as may be notified by the Central Government in the Official Gazette.

2. *Definitions*

1) In this Act, unless the context otherwise requires:

   a) "access" with its grammatical variations and cognate expressions means gaining entry into, instructing or communicating with the logical, arithmetical, or memory function resources of a computer, computer system or computer network;

b) "addressee" means a person who is intended by the originator to receive the electronic record but does not include any intermediary;

c) "adjudicating officer" means an adjudicating officer appointed under subsection (1) of section 46;

d) "affixing digital signature" with its grammatical variations and cognate expressions means adoption of any methodology or procedure by a person for the purpose of authenticating an electronic record by means of digital signature;

e) "appropriate Government" means as respects any matter:

   i) Enumerated in List II of the Seventh Schedule to the Constitution;

   ii) relating to any State law enacted under List III of the Seventh Schedule to the Constitution, the State Government and in any other case, the Central Government;

f) "asymmetric crypto system" means a system of a secure key pair consisting of a private key for creating a digital signature and a public key to verify the digital signature;

g) "Certifying Authority" means a person who has been granted a licence to issue a Digital Signature Certificate under section 24;

h) "certification practice statement" means a statement issued by a Certifying Authority to specify the practices that the Certifying Authority employs in issuing Digital Signature Certificates;

i) "computer" means any electronic magnetic, optical or other high-speed data processing device or system which performs logical, arithmetic, and memory functions by manipulations of electronic, magnetic or optical impulses, and includes all input, output, processing, storage, computer software, or communication facilities which are connected or related to the computer in a computer system or computer network;

j) "computer network" means the interconnection of one or more computers through

   i) the use of satellite, microwave, terrestrial line or other communication media; and

   ii) terminals or a complex consisting of two or more interconnected computers whether or not the interconnection is continuously maintained;

k) "computer resource" means computer, computer system, computer network, data, computer database or software;

l) "computer system" means a device or collection of devices, including input and output support devices and excluding calculators which are not programmable and capable of being used in conjunction with external files, which contain computer programmes, electronic instructions, input data and output data, that performs logic, arithmetic, data storage and retrieval, communication control and other functions;

m) "Controller" means the Controller of Certifying Authorities appointed under sub-section (l) of section 17;

n) "Cyber Appellate Tribunal" means the Cyber Regulations Appellate Tribunal established under sub-section (1) of section 48;

o) "data" means a representation of information, knowledge, facts, concepts or instructions which are being prepared or have been prepared in a formalised manner, and is intended to be processed, is being processed or has been processed in a computer system or computer network, and may be in any form (including computer printouts magnetic or optical storage media, punched cards, punched tapes) or stored internally in the memory of the computer;

p) "digital signature" means authentication of any electronic record by a subscriber by means of an electronic method or procedure in accordance with the provisions of section 3;

q) "Digital Signature Certificate" means a Digital Signature Certificate issued under sub-section (4) of section 35;

r) "electronic form" with reference to information means any information generated, sent, received or stored in media, magnetic, optical, computer memory, micro film, computer generated microfiche or similar device;

s) "Electronic Gazette" means the Official Gazette published in the electronic form;

t) "electronic record" means data, record or data generated, image or sound stored, received or sent in an electronic form or microfilm or computer generated microfiche;

u) "function", in relation to a computer, includes logic, control arithmetical process, deletion, storage and retrieval and communication or telecommunication from or within a computer;

v) "information" includes data, text, images, sound, voice, codes, computer programmes, software and databases or microfilm or computer generated micro-fiche:

w) "intermediary" with respect to any particular electronic message means any person who on behalf of another person receives, stores or transmits that message or provides any service with respect to that message;

x) "key pair", in an asymmetric crypto system, means a private key and its mathematically related public key, which are so related that the public key can verify a digital signature created by the private key;

y) "law" includes any Act of Parliament or of a State Legislature, Ordinances promulgated by the President or a Governor, as the case may be. Regulations made by the President under Article 240, Bills enacted as President's Act under sub-clause (a) of clause (1) of Article 357 of the Constitution and includes rules, regulations, bye-laws and orders issued or made thereunder;

z) "licence" means a licence granted to a Certifying Authority under section 24;

za) "originator" means a person who sends, generates, stores or transmits any electronic message or causes any electronic message to be sent, generated, stored or transmitted to any other person but does not include an inter-mediary;

zb) "prescribed" means prescribed by rules made under this Act;

zc) "private key" means the key of a key pair used to create a digital signature;

zd) "public key" means the key of a key pair used to verify a digital signature and listed in the Digital Signature Certificate;

ze) "secure system" means computer hardware, software, and procedure that:

  a) are reasonably secure from unauthorised access and misuse;

  b) provide a reasonable level of reliability and correct operation;

  c) are reasonably suited to performing the intended functions; and

  d) adhere to generally accepted security procedures;

zf) "security procedure" means the security procedure prescribed under section 16 by the Central Government;

zg) "subscriber" means a person in whose name the Digital Signature Certificate is issued;

zh) "verify" in relation to a digital signature, electronic record or public key, with its grammatical variations and cognate expressions means to determine whether

a) the initial electronic record was affixed with the digital signature by the use of private key corresponding to the public key of the subscriber;

b) the initial electronic record is retained intact or has been altered since such electronic record was so affixed with the digital signature.

2) Any reference in this Act to any enactment or any provision thereof shall, in relation to an area in which such enactment or such provision is not in force, be construed as a reference to the corresponding law or the relevant provision of the corresponding law, if any, in force in that area.

CHAPTER II

Digital Signature

3. *Authentication of electronic records*

1) Subject to the provisions of this section any subscriber may authenticate an electronic record by affixing his digital signature.

2) The authentication of the electronic record shall be effected by the use of asymmetric crypto system and hash function which envelop and transform the initial electronic record into another electronic record.

Explanation: For the purposes of this sub-section, "hash function" means an algorithm mapping or translation of one sequence of bits into another, generally smaller, set known as "hash result" such that an electronic record yields the same hash result every time the algorithm is executed with the same electronic record as its input making it computationally infeasible

a) to derive or reconstruct the original electronic record from the hash result produced by the algorithm;

b) that two electronic records can produce the same hash result using the algorithm.

3) Any person by the use of a public key of the subscriber can verify the electronic record.

4) The private key and the public key are unique to the subscriber and constitute a functioning key pair.

CHAPTER III

ELECTRONIC GOVERNANCE

4. Legal recognition of electronic records

Where any law provides that information or any other matter shall be in writing or in the typewritten or printed form, then, notwithstanding anything contained in such law, such requirement shall be deemed to have been satisfied if such information or matter is:

a) rendered or made available in an electronic form; and

b) accessible so as to be usable for a subsequent reference.

5. *Legal recognition of digital signatures*

Where any law provides that information or any other matter shall be authenticated by affixing the signature or any document shall be signed or bear the signature of any person, then, notwithstanding anything contained in such law, such requirement shall be deemed to have been satisfied, if such information or matter is authenticated by means of digital signature affixed in such manner as may be prescribed by the Central Government.

Explanation: For the purposes of this section, "signed", with its grammatical variations and cognate expressions, shall, with reference to a person, mean affixing of his handwritten signature or any mark on any document and the expression "signature" shall be construed accordingly.

6. *Use of electronic records and digital signatures in government and its agencies*

1) Where any law provides for

   a) the filing of any form application or any other document with any office, authority, body or agency owned or controlled by the appropriate Government in a particular manner;

   b) the issue or grant of any licence, permit, sanction or approval by whatever name called in a particular manner;

   c) the receipt or payment of money in a particular manner, then, notwithstanding anything contained in any other law for the time being in force, such requirement shall be deemed to have been satisfied if such filing, issue, grant, receipt or payment, as the case may be, is effected by means of such electronic form as may be prescribed by the appropriate Government.

2) The appropriate Government may, for the purposes of sub-section (1), by rules, prescribe:

a) the manner and format in which such electronic records shall be filed, created or issued;

b) the manner or method of payment of any fee or charges for filing, creation or issue any electronic record under clause (a).

7. Retention of electronic records

1) Where any law provides that documents, records or information shall be retained for any specific period, then, that requirement shall be deemed to have been satisfied if such documents, records or information are retained in the electronic form, if:

a) the information contained therein remains accessible so as to be usable for a subsequent reference;

b) the electronic record is retained in the format in which it was originally generated, sent or received or in a format which can be demonstrated to represent accurately the information originally generated, sent or received;

c) the details which will facilitate the identification of the origin, destination, date and time of despatch or receipt of such electronic record are available in the electronic record:

Provided that this clause does not apply to any information which is automatically generated solely for the purpose of enabling an electronic record to be despatched or received.

2) Nothing in this section shall apply to any law that expressly provides for the retention of documents, records or information in the form of electronic records.

8. Publication of rule, regulation, etc., in Electronic Gazette

Where any law provides that any rule, regulation, order, bye-law, notification or any other matter shall be published in the *Official Gazette,* then, such requirement shall be deemed to have been satisfied if such rule, regulation, order, bye-law, notification or any other matter is published in the *Official Gazette* or *Electronic Gazette:*

Provided that where any rule, regulation, order, bye-law, notification or any other matter is published in the *Official Gazette* or *Electronic Gazette,* the date of publication shall be deemed to be the date of the *Gazette* which was first published in any form.

9. Sections 6,7 and 8 not to confer right to insist document should be accepted in electronic form

Nothing contained in sections 6, 7 and 8 shall confer a right upon any person to insist that any Ministry or Department of the Central Government or the State Government or any authority or body established by or under any law or controlled or funded by the Central or State Government should accept, issue, create, retain and preserve any document in the form of electronic records or effect any monetary transaction in the electronic form.

10. Power to make rules by Central Government in respect of digital signature

The Central Government may, for the purposes of this Act, by rules, prescribe:

a) the type of digital signature;

b) the manner and format in which the digital signature shall be affixed;

c) the manner or procedure which facilitates identification of the person affixing the digital signature;

d) control processes and procedures to ensure adequate integrity, security and confidentiality of electronic records or payments; and

e) any other matter which is necessary to give legal effect to digital signatures.

CHAPTER IV

ATTRIBUTION ACKNOWLEDGEMENT AND DESPATCH OF ELECTRONIC RECORDS

1. Attribution of electronic records

An electronic record shall be attributed to the originator:

a) if it was sent by the originator himself;

b) by a person who had the authority to act on behalf of the originator in respect of that electronic record; or

c) by an information system programmed by or on behalf of the originator to operate automatically.

12. *Acknowledgement of receipt*

1) Where the originator has not agreed with the addressee that the acknowledgment of receipt of electronic record be given in a particular form or by a particular method, an acknowledgment may be given by:

   a) any communication by the addressee, automated or otherwise; or

   b) any conduct of the addressee, sufficient to indicate to the originator that the electronic record has been received.

2) Where the originator has stipulated that the electronic record shall be binding only on receipt of an acknowledgment of such electronic record by him, then unless acknowledgement has been so received, the electronic record shall be deemed to have been never sent by the originator.

3) Where the originator has not stipulated that the electronic record shall be binding only on receipt of such acknowledgement, and the acknowledgement has not been received by the originator within the time specified or agreed or, if no time has been specified or agreed to within a reasonable time, then the originator may give notice to the addressee stating that no acknowledgement has been received

by him and specifying a reasonable time by which the acknowledgement must be received by him and if no acknowledgement is received within the aforesaid time limit he may after giving notice to the addressee, treat the electronic record as though it has never been sent.

13. Time and place of despatch and receipt of electronic record

1) Save as otherwise agreed to between the originator and the addressee, the dispatch of an electronic record occurs when it enters a computer resource outside the control of the originator.

2) Save as otherwise agreed between the originator and the addressee, the time of receipt of an electronic record shall be determined as follows, namely:

    a) if the addressee has designated a computer resource for the purpose of receiving electronic records:

        i) receipt occurs at the time when the electronic, record enters the designated computer resource; or

        ii) if the electronic record is sent to a computer resource of the addressee that is not the designated computer resource, receipt occurs at the time when the electronic record is retrieved by the addressee;

    b) if the addressee has not designated a computer resource along with specified timings, if any, receipt occurs when the electronic record enters the computer resource of the addressee.

3) Save as otherwise agreed to between the originator and the addressee, an electronic record is deemed to be dispatched at the place where the originator has his place of business, and is deemed to be received at the place where the addressee has his place of business.

4) The provisions of sub-section (2) shall apply notwithstanding that the place where the computer resource is located may be different from the place where the electronic record is deemed to have been received under sub-section (3).

5) For the purposes of this section:

   a) if the originator or the addressee has more than one place of business, the principal place of business, shall be the place of business;

   b) if the originator or the addressee does not have a place of business, his usual place of residence shall be deemed to be the place of business;

   c) "usual place of residence", in relation to a body corporate, means the place where it is registered.

CHAPTER V

SECURE ELECTRONIC RECORD AND SECURE DIGITAL SIGNATURES

14. Secure electronic record

Where any security procedure has been applied to an electronic record at a specific point of time, then such record shall be deemed to be a secure electronic record from such point of time to the time of verification.

15. Secure digital signature

If, by application of a security procedure agreed to by the parties concerned, it can be verified that a digital signature, at the time it was affixed, was:

a) unique to the subscriber affixing it;

b) capable of identifying such subscriber;

c) created in a manner or using a means under the exclusive control of the subscriber and is linked to the electronic record to which it relates in such a manner that if the electronic record was altered the digital signature would be invalidated, then such digital signature shall be deemed to be a secure digital signature.

16. Security procedure

The Central Government shall for the purposes of this Act prescribe the security procedure having regard to commercial circumstances prevailing at the time when the procedure was used, including:

a) the nature of the transaction;

b) the level of sophistication of the parties with reference to their technological capacity;

c) the volume of similar transactions engaged in by other parties;

d) the availability of alternatives offered to but rejected by any party;

e) the cost of alternative procedures; and

f) the procedures in general use for similar types of transactions or communications.

CHAPTER VI

Regulation of Certifying Authorities

17. Appointment of controller and other officers

1) The Central Government may, by notification in the Official Gazette, appoint a Controller of Certifying Authorities for the purposes of this Act and may also by the same or subsequent notification appoint such number of Deputy Controllers and Assistant Controllers as it deems fit.
2) The Controller shall discharge his functions under this Act subject to the general control and directions of the Central Government.
3) The Deputy Controllers and Assistant Controllers shall perform the functions assigned to them by the Controller under the general superintendence and control of the Controller.
4) The qualifications, experience and terms and conditions of service of Controller, Deputy Controllers and Assistant Controllers shall be such as may be prescribed by the Central Government.
5) The Head Office and Branch Office of the office of the Controller shall be at such places as the Central Government may specify, and these may be established at such places as the Central Government may think fit.
6) There shall be a seal of the Office of the Controller.

18. Functions of controller

The Controller may perform all or any of the following functions, namely:

a) exercising supervision over the activities of the Certifying Authorities;

b) certifying public keys of the Certifying Authorities;

c) laying down the standards to be maintained by the Certifying Authorities;

d) specifying the qualifications and experience which employees of the Certifying Authorities should possess;

e) specifying the conditions subject to which the Certifying Authorities shall conduct their business;

f) specifying the contents of written, printed or visual materials and advertisements that may be distributed or used in respect of a Digital Signature Certificate and the public key;

g) specifying the form and content of a Digital Signature Certificate and the key,

h) specifying the form and manner in which accounts shall be maintained by the Certifying Authorities;

i) specifying the terms and conditions subject to which auditors may be appointed and the remuneration to be paid to them;

j) facilitating the establishment of any electronic system by a Certifying Authority either solely or jointly with other Certifying Authorities and regulation of such systems;

k) specifying the manner in which the Certifying Authorities shall conduct their dealings with the subscribers;

l) resolving any conflict of interests between the Certifying Authorities and the subscribers;

m) laying down the duties of the Certifying Authorities;

n) maintaining a data base containing the disclosure record of every Certifying Authority containing such particulars as may be specified by regulations, which shall be accessible to public.

19. Recognition of foreign certifying authorities

1) Subject to such conditions and restrictions as may be specified by regulations, the Controller may with the previous approval of the Central Government, and by notification in the Official Gazette, recognise any foreign Certifying Authority as a Certifying Authority for the purposes of this Act.

2) Where any Certifying Authority is recognised under sub-section (1), the Digital Signature Certificate issued by such Certifying Authority shall be valid for the purposes of this Act.

3) The Controller may, if he is satisfied that any Certifying Authority has contravened any of the conditions and restrictions subject to which it was granted recognition under sub-section (1) he may, for reasons to be recorded in writing, by notification in the Official Gazette, revoke such recognition.

20. Controller to act as repository

1) The Controller shall be the repository of all Digital Signature Certificates issued under this Act.

2) The Controller shall:

   a) make use of hardware, software and procedures that are secure from intrusion and misuse;

   b) observe such other standards as may be prescribed by the Central Government, to ensure that the secrecy and security of the digital signatures are assured.

3) The Controller shall maintain a computerised database of all public keys in such a manner that such database and the public keys are available to any member of the public.

21. Licence to issue digital signature certificates

1) Subject to the provisions of sub-section (2), any person may make an application, to the Controller, for a licence to issue Digital Signature Certificates.

2) No licence shall be issued under sub-section (1), unless the applicant fulfils such requirements with respect to qualification, expertise, manpower, financial resources and other infrastructure facilities, which are necessary to issue Digital Signature Certificates as may be prescribed by the Central Government.

3) A licence granted under this section shall:

   a) be valid for such period as may be prescribed by the Central Government;

   b) not be transferable or heritable;

   c) be subject to such terms and conditions as may be specified by the regulations.

22. *Application for licence*

1) Every application for issue of a licence shall be in such form as may be prescribed by the Central Government.

2) Every application for issue of a licence shall be accompanied by:

   a) a certification practice statement;

   b) a statement including the procedures with respect to identification of the applicant;

   c) payment of such fees, not exceeding twenty-five thousand rupees as may be prescribed by the Central Government;

   d) such other documents, as may be prescribed by the Central Government.

23. *Renewal of licence*

An application for renewal of a licence shall be:

a) in such form;

b) accompanied by such fees, not exceeding five thousand rupees, as may be prescribed by the Central Government and shall be made not less than forty-five days before the date of expiry of the period of validity of the licence.

24. *Procedure for grant or rejection of licence*

The Controller may, on receipt of an application under sub-section (1) of section 21, after considering the documents accompanying the application and such other factors, as he deems fit, grant the licence or reject the application:

Provided that no application shall be rejected under this section unless the applicant has been given a reasonable opportunity of presenting his case.

25. *Suspension of licence*

1) The Controller may, if he is satisfied after making such inquiry, as he may think fit, that a Certifying Authority has:

   a) made a statement in, or in relation to, the application for the issue or renewal of the licence, which is incorrect or false in material particulars;

   b) failed to comply with the terms and conditions subject to which the licence was granted;

   c) failed to maintain the standards specified under clause (b) of sub-section (2) of section 20;

   d) contravened any provisions of this Act, rule, regulation or order made thereunder,

Revoke the licence

Provided that no licence shall be revoked unless the Certifying Authority has been given a reasonable opportunity of showing cause against the proposed revocation.

2) The Controller may, if he has reasonable cause to believe that there is any ground for revoking a licence under sub-section (1), by order suspend such licence pending the completion of any inquiry ordered by him:

Provided that no licence shall be suspended for a period exceeding ten days unless the Certifying Authority has been given a reasonable opportunity of showing cause against the proposed suspension.

3) No Certifying Authority whose licence has been suspended shall issue any Digital Signature Certificate during such suspension.

26. *Notice of suspension or revocation of licence*

1) Where the licence of the Certifying Authority is suspended or revoked, the Controller shall publish notice of such suspension or revocation, as the case may be, in the database maintained by him.

2) Where one or more repositories are specified, the Controller shall publish notices of such suspension or revocation, as the case may be, in all such repositories:

   Provided that the database containing the notice of such suspension or revocation, as the case may be, shall be made available through a website which shall be accessible round the clock:

   Provided further that the Controller may, if he considers necessary, publicise the contents of database in such electronic or other media, as he may consider appropriate.

27. *Power to delegate*

The Controller may, in writing, authorise the Deputy Controller, Assistant Controller or any officer to exercise any of the powers of the Controller under this Chapter.

28. *Power to investigate contraventions*

1) The Controller or any officer authorised by him in this behalf shall take up for investigation any contravention of the provisions of this Act, rules or regulations made thereunder.

2) The Controller or any officer authorised by him in this behalf shall exercise the like powers which are conferred on Income-tax authorities under Chapter XIII of the Income-tax Act, 1961 and shall exercise such powers, subject to such limitations laid down under that Act.

29. *Access to computers and data*

1) Without prejudice to the provisions of sub-section (1) of section 69, the Controller or any person authorised by him shall, if he has reasonable cause to suspect that any contravention of the provisions of this Act, rules or regulations made thereunder has been committed, have access to any computer system, any apparatus, data or any other material connected with such system, for the purpose of searching or causing a search to be made for obtaining any information or data contained in or available to such computer system.

2) For the purposes of sub-section (1), the Controller or any person authorised by him may, by order, direct any person in charge of, or otherwise concerned with the operation of, the computer system, data apparatus or material, to provide him with such reasonable technical and other assistance as he may consider necessary.

30. Certifying authority to follow certain procedures

Every Certifying Authority shall:

a) make use of hardware, software and procedures that are secure from intrusion and misuse;

b) provide a reasonable level of reliability in its services which are reasonably suited to the performance of intended functions;

c) adhere to security procedures to ensure that the secrecy and privacy of the digital signatures are assured; and

d) observe such other standards as may be specified by regulations.

31. Certifying authority to ensure compliance of the Act, etc.

Every Certifying Authority shall ensure that every person employed or otherwise engaged by it complies, in the course of his employment or engagement, with the provisions of this Act, rules, regulations and orders made thereunder.

32. Display of licence

Every Certifying Authority shall display its licence at a conspicuous place of the premises in which it carries on its business.

33. Surrender of licence

1) Every Certifying Authority whose licence is suspended or revoked shall immediately after such

suspension or revocation, surrender the licence to the Controller.

2) Where any Certifying Authority fails to surrender a licence under sub-section (1), the person in whose favour a licence is issued, shall be guilty of an offence and shall be punished with imprisonment which may extend up to six months or a fine which may extend up to ten thousand rupees or with both.

34. *Disclosure*

1) Every Certifying Authority shall disclose in the manner specified by regulations:

   a) its Digital Signature Certificate which contains the public key corresponding to the private key used by that Certifying Authority to digitally sign another Digital Signature Certificate;

   b) any certification practice statement relevant thereto;

   c) notice of the revocation or suspension of its Certifying Authority certificate, if any; and

   d) any other fact that materially and adversely affects either the reliability of a Digital Signature Certificate, which that Authority has issued, or the Authority's ability to perform its services.

2) Wherein the opinion of the Certifying Authority any event has occurred or any situation has arisen which may materially and adversely affect the integrity of its computer system or the conditions subject to which a Digital Signature Certificate was granted, then, the Certifying Authority shall:

a) use reasonable efforts to notify any person who is likely to be affected by that occurrence; or

b) act in accordance with the procedure specified in its certification practice statement to deal with such event or situation.

CHAPTER VII

DIGITAL SIGNATURE CERTIFICATES

35. Certifying authority to issue digital signature certificate

1) Any person may make an application to the Certifying Authority for the issue of a Digital Signature Certificate in such form as may be prescribed by the Central Govern-ment.

2) Every such application shall be accompanied by such fee not exceeding twenty-five thousand rupees as may be prescribed by the Central Government, to be paid to the Certifying Authority:

   Provided that while prescribing fees under sub-section (2) different fees may be prescribed for different classes of applicants.

3) Every such application shall be accompanied by a certification practice statement or where there is no such statement, a statement containing such particulars, as may be specified by regulations.

4) On receipt of an application under sub-section (1), the Certifying Authority may, after consideration of the certification practice statement or the other statement under sub-section (3) and after making

such enquiries as it may deem fit, grant the Digital Signature Certificate or for reasons to be recorded in writing, reject the application:

Provided that no Digital Signature Certificate shall be granted unless the Certifying Authority is satisfied that:

a) the applicant holds the private key corresponding to the public key to be listed in the Digital Signature Certificate;

b) the applicant holds a private key, which is capable of creating a digital signature;

c) the public key to be listed in the certificate can be used to verify a digital signature affixed by the private key held by the applicant:

Provided further that no application shall be rejected unless the applicant has been given a reasonable opportunity of showing cause against the proposed rejection.

36. Representations upon issuance of digital signature certificate

A Certifying Authority while issuing a Digital Signature Certificate shall certify that:

a) it has complied with the provisions of this Act and the rules and regulations made thereunder,

b) it has published the Digital Signature Certificate or otherwise made it available to such person relying on it and the subscriber has accepted it;

c) the subscriber holds the private key corresponding to the public key, listed in the Digital Signature Certificate;

d) the subscriber's public key and private key constitute a functioning key pair,

e) the information contained in the Digital Signature Certificate is accurate; and

f) it has no knowledge of any material fact, which if it had been included in the Digital Signature Certificate would adversely affect the reliability of the representations made in clauses (a) to (d).

37. *Suspension of digital signature certificate*

1) Subject to the provisions of sub-section (2), the Certifying Authority which has issued a Digital Signature Certificate may suspend such Digital Signature Certificate:

   a) on receipt of a request to that effect from:

      i) the subscriber listed in toe Digital Signature Certificate; or

      ii) any person duly authorised to act on behalf of that subscriber.

   b) if it is of opinion that the Digital Signature Certificate should be suspended in public interest.

2) A Digital Signature Certificate shall not be suspended for a period exceeding fifteen days unless the subscriber has been given an opportunity of being heard in the matter.

3) On suspension of a Digital Signature Certificate under this section, the Certifying Authority shall communicate the same to the subscriber.

38. *Revocation of digital signature certificate*

1) A Certifying Authority may revoke a Digital Signature Certificate issued by it:

   a) where the subscriber or any other person authorised by him makes a request to that effect; or

   b) upon the death of the subscriber, or

   c) upon the dissolution of the firm or winding up of the company where the subscriber is a firm or a company.

2) Subject to the provisions of sub-section (3) and without prejudice to the provisions of sub-section (1), a Certifying Authority may revoke a Digital Signature Certificate which has been issued by it at any time, if it is of opinion that:

   a) a material fact represented in the Digital Signature Certificate is false or has been concealed;

   b) a requirement for issuance of the Digital Signature Certificate was not satisfied;

   c) the Certifying Authority's private key or security system was compromised in a manner materially affecting the Digital Signature Certificate's reliability;

   d) the subscriber has been declared insolvent or dead or where a subscriber is a firm or a company, which has been dissolved, wound-up or otherwise ceased to exist.

3) A Digital Signature Certificate shall not be revoked unless the subscriber has been given an opportunity of being heard in the matter.

4) On revocation of a Digital Signature Certificate under this section, the Certifying Authority shall communicate the same to the subscriber.

39. *Notice of suspension or revocation*

1) Where a Digital Signature Certificate is suspended or revoked under section 37 or section 38, the Certifying Authority shall publish a notice of such suspension or revocation, as the case may be, in the repository specified in the Digital Signature Certificate for publication of such notice.

2) Where one or more repositories are specified, the Certifying Authority shall publish notices of such suspension or revocation, as the case may be in all such repositories.

CHAPTER VIII

Duties of Subscribers

40. *Generating key pair*

Where any Digital Signature Certificate, the public key of which corresponds to the private key of that subscriber which is to be listed in the Digital Signature Certificate has been accepted by a subscriber, then, the subscriber shall generate the key pair by applying the security procedure.

41. Acceptance of digital signature certificate

1) A subscriber shall be deemed to have accepted a Digital Signature Certificate if he publishes or authorises the publication of a Digital Signature Certificate:

   a) to one or more persons;

   b) in a repository, or otherwise demonstrates his approval of the Digital Signature Certificate in any manner.

2) By accepting a Digital Signature Certificate the subscriber certifies to all who reasonably rely on the information contained in the Digital Signature Certificate that:

   a) the subscriber holds the private key corresponding to the public key listed in the Digital Signature Certificate and is entitled to hold the same;

   b) all representations made by the subscriber to the Certifying Authority and all material relevant to the information contained in the Digital Signature Certificate are true;

   c) all information in the Digital Signature Certificate that is within the knowledge of the subscriber is true.

42. Control of private key

1) Every subscriber shall exercise reasonable care to retain control of the private key corresponding to the public key listed in his Digital Signature Certificate and take all steps to prevent its disclosure to a

person not authorised to affix the digital signature of the subscriber.

2) If the private key corresponding to the public key listed in the Digital Signature Certificate has been compromised, then, the subscriber shall communicate the same without any delay to the Certifying Authority in such manner as may be specified by the regulations.

Explanation: For the removal of doubts, it is hereby declared that the subscriber shall be liable till he has informed the Certifying Authority that the private key has been compromised.

CHAPTER IX

Penalties and Adjudication

43. *Penalty for damage to computer, computer system, etc.*

If any person without permission of the owner or any other person who is incharge of a computer, computer system or computer network:

a) accesses or secures access to such computer, computer system or computer network;

b) downloads, copies or extracts any data, computer database or information from such computer, computer system or computer network including information or data held or stored in any removable storage medium;

c) introduces or causes to be introduced any computer contaminant or computer virus into any computer, computer system or computer network;

d) damages or causes to be damaged any computer, computer system or computer network, data, computer database or any other programmes residing in such computer, computer system or computer network;

e) disrupts or causes disruption of any computer, computer system or computer network;

f) denies or causes the denial of access to any person authorised to access any computer, computer system or computer network by any means;

g) provides any assistance to any person to facilitate access to a computer, computer system or computer network in contravention of the provisions of this Act, rules or regulations made thereunder;

h) charges the services availed of by a person to the account of another person by tampering with or manipulating any computer, computer system, or computer network, he shall be liable to pay damages by way of compensation not exceeding one crore rupees to the person so affected.

Explanation: For the purposes of this section:

i) "computer contaminant" means any set of computer instructions that are designed:

   a) to modify, destroy, record, transmit data or pro-gramme residing within a computer, computer system or computer network; or

   b) by any means to usurp the normal operation of the computer, computer system, or computer network;

ii) "computer database" means a representation of information, knowledge, facts, concepts or instructions in text, image, audio, video that are being prepared or have been prepared in a formalised manner or have been produced by a computer, computer system or computer network and are intended for use in a computer, computer system or computer network;

iii) "computer virus" means any computer instruction, information, data or programme that destroys, damages, degrades or adversely affects the performance of a computer resource or attaches itself to another computer resource and operates when a programme, daia or instruction is executed or some other event takes place in that computer resource;

iv) "damage" means to destroy, alter, delete, add, modify or rearrange any computer resource by any means.

44. Penalty for failure to furnish information return, etc.

If any person who is required under this Act or any rules or regulations made thereunder to:

a) furnish any document, return or report to the Controller or the Certifying Authority fails to furnish the same, he shall be liable to a penalty not exceeding one lakh and fifty thousand rupees for each such failure;

b) file any return or furnish any information, books or other documents within the time specified therefor in the regulations fails to file return or furnish the same within the time specified therefore in the regulations, he shall be liable to a penalty not exceeding five thousand rupees for every day during which such failure continues;

c) maintain books of account or records, fails to maintain the same, he shall be liable to a penalty not exceeding ten thousand rupees for every day during which the failure continues.

45. Residuary penalty

Whoever contravenes any rules or regulations made under this Act, for the contravention of which no penalty has been separately provided, shall be liable to pay a compensation not exceeding twenty-five thousand rupees to the person affected by such contravention or a penalty not exceeding twenty-five thousand rupees.

46. Power to adjudicate

1) For the purpose of adjudging under this Chapter whether any person has committed a contravention of any of the provisions of this Act or of any rule, regulation, direction or order made thereunder the Central Government shall, subject to the provisions of sub-section (3), appoint any officer not below the rank of a Director to the Government of India or an equivalent officer of a State Government to be an adjudicating officer for holding an inquiry in the manner prescribed by the Central Government.

2) The adjudicating officer shall, after giving the person referred to in sub-section (1) a reasonable

opportunity for making representation in the matter and if, on such inquiry, he is satisfied that the person has committed the contravention, he may impose such penalty or award such compensation as he thinks fit in accordance with the provisions of that section.

3) No person shall be appointed as an adjudicating officer unless he possesses such experience in the field of Information Technology and legal or judicial experience as may be prescribed by the Central Government.

4) Where more than one adjudicating officers are appointed, the Central Government shall specify by order the matters and places with respect to which such officers shall exercise their jurisdiction.

5) Every adjudicating officer shall have the powers of a civil court which are conferred oh the Cyber Appellate Tribunal under sub-section (2) of section 58, and:

   a) all proceedings before it shall be deemed to be judicial proceedings within the meaning of sections 193 and 228 of the Indian Penal Code;

   b) shall be deemed to be a civil court for the purposes of sections 345 and 346 of the Code of Criminal Procedure, 1973.

47. Factors to be taken into account by the adjudicating officer

While adjudging the quantum of compensation under this Chapter, the adjudicating officer shall have due regard to the following factors, namely:

a) the amount of gain of unfair advantage, wherever quantifiable, made as a result of the default;
b) the amount of loss caused to any person as a result of the default;
c) the repetitive nature of the default.

CHAPTER X

The Cyber Regulations Appellate Tribunal

48. Establishment of cyber appellate tribunal

1) The Central Government shall, by notification, establish one or more appellate tribunals to be known as the Cyber Regulations Appellate Tribunal.
2) The Central Government shall also specify, in the notification referred to in sub-section (1), the matters and places in relation to which the Cyber Appellate Tribunal may exercise jurisdiction.

49. Composition of cyber appellate tribunal

A Cyber Appellate Tribunal shall consist of one person only (hereinafter referred to as the Residing Officer of the Cyber Appellate Tribunal) to be appointed, by notification, by the Central Government.

50. Qualifications for appointment as presiding officer of the Cyber Appellate Tribunal

A person shall not be qualified for appointment as the Presiding Officer of a Cyber Appellate Tribunal unless he:

a) is, or has been or is qualified to be, a Judge of a High Court; or

b) is or has been a member of the Indian Legal Service and is holding or has held a post in Grade I of that Service for at least three years.

51. *Term of office*

The Presiding Officer of a Cyber Appellate Tribunal shall hold office for a term of five years from the date on which he enters upon his office or until he attains the age of sixty-five years, whichever is earlier.

52. *Salary, allowances and other terms and conditions of service of presiding officer*

The salary and allowances payable to, and the other terms and conditions of service including pension, gratuity and other retirement benefits of the Presiding Officer of a Cyber Appellate Tribunal shall be such as may be prescribed:

> Provided that neither the salary and allowances nor the other terms and conditions of service of the Presiding Officer shall be varied to his disadvantage after appointment.

53. *Filling up of vacancies*

If, for reason other than temporary absence, any vacancy occurs in the office of the Presiding Officer of a Cyber Appellate Tribunal, then the Central Government shall appoint another person in accordance with the provisions of this Act to fill the vacancy and the proceedings may be continued before the Cyber Appellate Tribunal from the stage at which the vacancy is filled.

54. *Resignation and removal*

1) The Presiding Officer of a Cyber Appellate Tribunal may, by notice in writing under his hand addressed to the Central Government, resign his office:

   Provided that the said Presiding Officer shall, unless he is permitted by the Central Government to relinquish his office sooner, continue to hold office until the expiry of three months from the date of receipt of such notice or until a person duly appointed as his successor enters upon his office or until the expiry of his term of office, whichever is the earliest.

2) The Presiding Officer of a Cyber Appellate Tribunal shall not be removed from his office except by an order by the Central Government on the ground of proved misbehaviour or incapacity after an inquiry made by a Judge of the Supreme Court in which the Presiding Officer concerned has been informed of the charges against him and given a reasonable opportunity of being heard in respect of these charges.

3) The Central Government may, by rules, regulate the procedure for the investigation of misbehaviour or incapacity of the aforesaid Presiding Officer.

55. *Orders constituting Appellate Tribunal to be final and not to invalidate its proceedings*

No order of the Central Government appointing any person as the Presiding Officer of a Cyber Appellate Tribunal shall be called in question in any manner and no act or proceeding before a Cyber Appellate Tribunal shall be called in question in any manner on the ground merely of any defect in the constitution of a Cyber Appellate Tribunal.

56. *Staff of the cyber appellate tribunal*

1) The Central Government shall provide the Cyber Appellate Tribunal with such officers and employees as that Government may think fit.

2) The officers and employees of the Cyber Appellate Tribunal shall discharge their functions under general superintendence of the Presiding Officer.

3) The salaries, allowances and other conditions of service of the officers and employees or the Cyber Appellate Tribunal shall be such as may be prescribed by the Central Govern-ment.

57. *Appeal to cyber appellate tribunal*

1) Save as provided in sub-section (2), any person aggrieved by an order made by Controller or an adjudicating officer under this Act may prefer an appeal to a Cyber Appellate Tribunal having jurisdiction in the matter.

2) No appeal shall lie to the Cyber Appellate Tribunal from an order made by an adjudicating officer with the consent of the parties.

3) Every appeal under sub-section (1) shall be filed within a period of twenty-five days from the date on which a copy of the order made by the Controller or the adjudicating officer is received by the person

aggrieved and it shall be in such form and be accompanied by such fee as may be prescribed:

Provided that the Cyber Appellate Tribunal may entertain an appeal after the expiry of the said period of twenty-five days if it is satisfied that there was sufficient cause tor not filing it within that period.

4) On receipt of an appeal under sub-section (1), the Cyber Appellate Tribunal may, after giving the parties to the appeal, an opportunity of being heard, pass such orders thereon as it thinks fit, confirming, modifying or setting aside the order appealed against.

5) The Cyber Appellate Tribunal shall send a copy of every order made by it to the parties to the appeal and to the concerned Controller or adjudicating officer.

6) The appeal filed before the Cyber Appellate Tribunal under sub-section (1) shall be dealt with by it as expeditiously as possible and endeavour shall be made by it to dispose of the appeal finally within six months from the date of receipt of the appeal.

58. Procedure and powers of the cyber appellate tribunal

1) The Cyber Appellate Tribunal shall not be bound by the procedure laid down by the Code of civil Procedure, 1908 but shall be guided by the principles of natural justice and, subject to the other provisions of this Act and of any rules, the Cyber Appellate Tribunal shall have powers to regulate its own procedure including the place at which it shall have its sittings.

2) The Cyber Appellate Tribunal shall have, for the purposes of discharging its functions under this Act, the same powers as are vested in a civil court under the Code of Civil Procedure, 1908, while trying a suit, in respect of the following matters, namely:

   a) summoning and enforcing the attendance of any person and examining him on oath;

   b) requiring the discovery and production of documents or other electronic records;

   c) receiving evidence on affidavits;

   d) issuing commissions for the examination of witnesses or documents;

   e) reviewing its decisions;

   f) dismissing an application for default or deciding it *ex pane;*

   g) any other matter which may be prescribed.

3) Every proceeding before the Cyber Appellate Tribunal shall be deemed to be a judicial proceeding within the meaning of sections 193 and 228, and for the purposes of section 196 of the Indian Penal Code and the Cyber Appellate Tribunal shall be deemed to be a civil court for the purposes of section 195 and Chapter XXVI of the Code of Criminal Procedure, 1973.

59. Right to legal representation

The appellant may either appear in person or authorise one or more legal practitioners or any of its officers to present his or its case before the Cyber Appellate Tribunal.

60. Limitation

The provisions of the Limitation Act, 1963, shall, as far as may be, apply to an appeal made to the Cyber Appellate Tribunal.

61. Civil court not to have jurisdiction

No court shall have jurisdiction to entertain any suit or proceeding in respect of any matter which an adjudicating officer appointed under this Act or the Cyber Appellate Tribunal constituted under this Act is empowered by or under this Act to determine and no injunction shall be granted by any court or other authority in respect of any action taken or to be taken in pursuance of any power conferred by or under this Act.

62. Appeal to high court

Any person aggrieved by any decision or order of the Cyber Appellate Tribunal may file an appeal to the High Court within sixty days from the date of communication of the decision or order of the Cyber Appellate Tribunal to him on any question of fact or law arising out of such order.

Provided that the High Court may, if it is satisfied that the appellant was prevented by sufficient cause from filing the appeal within the said period, allow it to be filed within a further period not exceeding sixty days.

63. Compounding of contraventions

1) Any contravention under this Chapter may, either before or after the institution of adjudication

proceedings, be compounded by the Controller or such other officer as may be specially authorised by him in this behalf or by the adjudicating officer, as the case may be, subject to such conditions as the Controller or such other officer or the adjudicating officer may specify:

Provided that such sum shall not, in any case, exceed the maximum amount of the penalty which may be imposed under this Act for the contravention so compounded.

2) Nothing in sub-section (1) shall apply to a person who commits the same or similar contravention within a period of three years from the date on which the first contravention, committed by him, was compounded.

Explanation: For the purposes of this sub-section, any second or subsequent contravention committed after the expiry of a period of three years from the date on which the contravention was previously compounded shall be deemed to be a first contravention.

3) Where any contravention has been compounded under sub-section (1), no proceeding or further proceeding, as the case may be, shall be taken against the person guilty of such contravention in respect of the contravention so compounded.

64. *Recovery of penalty*

A penalty imposed under this Act, if it is not paid, shall be recovered as an area of land revenue and the licence or the Digital Signature Certificate, as the case may be, shall be suspended till the penalty is paid.

CHAPTER XI

OFFENCES

65. Tampering with computer source documents

Whoever knowingly or intentionally conceals, destroys or alters or intentionally or knowingly causes another to conceal, destroy or alter any computer source code used for a computer, computer programme, computer system or computer network, when the computer source code is required to be kept or maintained by law for the time being in force, shall be punishable with imprisonment up to three years, or with fine which may extend up to two lakh rupees, or with both.

Explanation.—For the purposes of this section, 'computer source code' means the listing of programmes, computer commands, design and layout and programme analysis of computer resource in any form.

66. Hacking with computer system

1) Whoever with the intent to cause or knowing that he is likely to cause wrongful loss or damage to the public or any person destroys or deletes or alters any information residing in a computer resource or diminishes its value or utility or affects it injuriously by any means, commits hack:

2) Whoever commits hacking shall be punished with imprisonment up to three years, or with fine which may extend upto two lakh rupees, or with both.

67. Publishing of information which is obscene in electronic form

Whoever publishes or transmits or causes to be published in the electronic form, any material which is lascivious or appeals to the prurient interest or if its effect is such as to tend to deprave and corrupt persons who are likely, having regard to all relevant circumstances, to read, see or hear the matter contained or embodied in it, shall be punished on first conviction with imprisonment of either description for a term which may extend to five years and with fine which may extend to one lakh rupees and in the event of a second or subsequent conviction with imprisonment of either description for a term which may extend to ten years and also with fine which may extend to two lakh rupees.

68. Power of Controller to give directions

1) The Controller may, by order, direct a Certifying Authority or any employee of such Authority to take such measures or cease carrying on such activities as specified in the order if those are necessary to ensure compliance with the provisions of this Act, rules or any regulations made thereunder.

2) Any person who fails to comply with any order under sub-section (1) shall be guilty of an offence and shall be liable on conviction to imprisonment for a term not exceeding three years or to a fine not exceeding two lakh rupees or to both.

69. Directions of Controller to a subscriber to extend facilities to decrypt information

1) If the Controller is satisfied that it is necessary or expedient so to do in the interest of the sovereignty or integrity of India, the security of the State, friendly relations with foreign Stales or public order or for preventing incitement to the commission of any cognizable offence, for reasons to be recorded in writing, by order, direct any agency of the Government to intercept any information transmitted through any computer resource.
2) The subscriber or any person incharge of the computer resource shall, when called upon by any agency which has been directed under sub-section (1), extend all facilities and technical assistance to decrypt the information.
3) The subscriber or any person who fails to assist the agency referred to in sub-section (2) shall be punished with an imprisonment for a term which may extend to seven years.

70. Protected system

1) The appropriate Government may, by notification in the *Official Gazette*, declare that any computer, computer system or computer network to be a protected system.
2) The appropriate Government may, by order in writing, authorise the persons who are authorised to access protected systems notified under sub-section (1).

3) Any person who secures access or attempts to secure access to a protected system in contravention of the provisions of this section shall be punished with imprisonment of either description for a term which may extend to ten years and shall also be liable to fine.

71. Penalty for misrepresentation

Whoever makes any misrepresentation to, or suppresses any material fact from, the Controller or the Certifying Authority for obtaining any licence or Digital Signature Certificate, as the case may be shall be punished with imprisonment for a term which may extend to two years, or with fine which may extend to one lakh rupees, or with both.

72. Penalty for breach of confidentiality and privacy

Save as otherwise provided in this Act or any other law for the time being in force, any person who, in pursuance of any of the powers conferred under this Act, rules or regulations made thereunder, has secured access to any electronic record, book, register, correspondence, information, document or other material without the consent of the person concerned discloses such electronic record, book, register, correspondence, information, document or other material to any other person shall be punished with imprisonment for a term which may extend to two years, or with fine which may extend to one lakh rupees, or with both.

73. Penalty for publishing Digital Signature Certificate false in certain particulars

1) No person shall publish a Digital Signature Certificate or otherwise make it available to any other person with the knowledge that:

   a) the Certifying Authority listed in the certificate has not issued it; or

   b) the subscriber listed in the certificate has not accepted it; or

   c) the certificate has been revoked or suspended, unless such publication is for the purpose of verifying a digital signature created prior to such suspension or revocation.

2) Any person who contravenes the provisions of sub-section (1) shall be punished with imprisonment for a term which may extend to two years, or with fine which may extend to one lakh rupees, or with both.

74. Publication for fraudulent purpose

Whoever knowingly creates, publishes or otherwise makes available a Digital Signature Certificate for any fraudulent or unlawful purpose shall be punished with imprisonment for a term which may extend to two years, or with fine which may extend to one lakh rupees, or with both.

75. Act to apply for offence or contravention committed outside India

1) Subject to the provisions of sub-section (2), the provisions of this Act shall apply also to any offence

or contravention committed outside India by any person irrespective of his nationality.

2) For the purposes of sub-section (1), this Act shall apply to an offence or contravention committed outside India by any person if the act or conduct constituting the offence or contravention involves a computer, computer system or computer network located in India.

76. Confiscation

Any computer, computer system, floppies, compact disks, tape drives or any other accessories related thereto, in respect of which any provision of this Act, rules, orders or regulations made thereunder has been or is being contravened, shall be liable to confiscation:

Provided that where it is established to the satisfaction of the court adjudicating the confiscation that the person in whose possession, power or control of any such computer, computer system, floppies, compact disks, tape drives or any other accessories relating thereto is found is not responsible for the contravention of the provisions of this Act, rules, orders or regulations made thereunder, the court may, instead of making an order for confiscation of such computer, computer system, floppies, compact disks, tape drives or any other accessories related thereto, make such other order authorised by this Act against the person contravening of the provisions of this Act, rules, orders or regulations made thereunder as it may think fit.

77. Penalties or confiscation not to interfere with other punishments

No penalty imposed or confiscation made under this Act shall prevent the imposition of any other punishment to which the person affected thereby is liable under any other law for the time being in force.

78. Power to investigate offences

Notwithstanding anything contained in the Code of Criminal Procedure, 1973, a police officer not below the rank of Deputy Superintendent of Police shall investigate any offence under this Act.

CHAPTER XII

NETWORK SERVICE PROVIDERS NOT TO BE LIABLE IN CERTAIN CASES

79. Network service providers not to be liable in certain cases

For the removal of doubts, it is hereby declared that no person providing any service as a network service provider shall be liable under this Act, rules or regulations made thereunder for any third party information or data made available by him if he proves that the offence or contravention was committed without his knowledge or that he had exercised all due diligence to prevent the commission of such offence or contravention.

Explanation: For the purposes of this section:

a) "network service provider" means an intermediary;

b) "third party information" means any information dealt with by a network service provider in his capacity as an intermediary.

CHAPTER XIII

MISCELLANEOUS

80. Power of police officer and other officers to enter, search, etc.

1) Notwithstanding anything contained in the Code of Criminal Procedure, 1973, any police officer, not below the rank of a Deputy Superintendent of Police, or any other officer of the Central Government or a State Government authorised by the Central Government in this behalf may enter any public place and search and arrest without warrant any person found therein who is reasonably suspected or having committed or of committing or of being about to commit any offence under this Act

   Explanation: For the purposes of this sub-section, the expression "public place" includes any public conveyance, any hotel, any shop or any other place intended for use by, or accessible to the public.

2) Where any person is arrested under sub-section (1) by an officer other than a police officer, such officer shall, without unnecessary delay, take or send the person arrested before a magistrate having jurisdiction in the case or before the officer-in-charge of a police station.

3) The provisions of the Code of Criminal Procedure, 1973 shall, subject to the provisions of this section,

apply, so far as may be, in relation to any entry, search or arrest, made under this section.

81. Act to have overriding effect

The provisions of this Act shall have effect notwithstanding anything inconsistent therewith contained in any other law for the time being in force.

82. Controller, deputy controller and assistant controllers to be public servants

The Presiding Officer and other officers and employees of a Cyber Appellate Tribunal, the Controller, the Deputy Controller and the Assistant Controllers shall be deemed to be public servants within the meaning of section 21 of the Indian Penal Code.

83. Power to give directions

The Central Government may give directions to any State Government as to the carrying into execution in the State of any of the provisions of this Act or of any rule, regulation or order made thereunder.

84. Protection of action taken in good faith

No suit, prosecution or other legal proceeding shall lie against the Central Government, the State Government, the Controller or any person acting on behalf of him, the Presiding Officer, adjudicating officers and the staff of the Cyber Appellate Tribunal for anything which is in good faith done or intended to be done in pursuance of this Act or any rule, regulation or order made thereunder.

85. Offences by companies

1) Where a person committing a contravention of any of the provisions of this Act or of any rule, direction or order made thereunder is a company, every person who, at the time the contravention was committed, was in charge of, and was responsible to, the company for the conduct of business of the company as well as the company, shall be guilty of the contravention and shall be liable to be proceeded against and punished accordingly:

   Provided that nothing contained in this sub-section shall render any such person liable to punishment if he proves that the contravention took place without his knowledge or that he exercised all due diligence to prevent such contravention.

2) Notwithstanding anything contained in sub-section (1), where a contravention of any of the provisions of this Act or of any rule, direction or order made thereunder has been committed by a company and it is proved that the contravention has taken place with the consent or connivance of, or is attributable to any neglect on the part of, any director, manager, secretary or other officer of the company, such director, manager, secretary or other officer shall also be deemed to be guilty of the contravention and shall be liable to be proceeded against and punished accordingly.

   Explanation: For the purposes of this section:

   i) "company" means any body corporate and includes a firm or other association of individuals; and

ii) "director", in relation to a firm, means a partner in the firm.

86. Removal of difficulties

1) If any difficulty arises in giving effect to the provisions of this Act, the Central Government may, by order published in the *Official Gazette*, make such provisions not inconsistent with the provisions of this Act as appear to it to be necessary or expedient for removing the difficulty:

Provided that no order shall be made under this section after the expiry of a period of two years from the commencement of this Act.

2) Every order made under this section shall be laid, as soon as may be after it is made, before each House of Parliament.

87. Power of central government to make rules

1) The Central Government may, by notification in the *Official Gazette* and in the *Electronic Gazette* make rules to carry out the provisions of this Act

2) In particular, and without prejudice to the generality of the foregoing power, such rules may provide for all or any of the following mailers, namely:

   a) the manner in which any information or matter may be authenticated by means of digital signature under section 5;

   b) the electronic form in which filing, issue, grant or payment shall be effected under sub-section (1) of section 6;

c) the manner and format in which electronic records shall be filed, or issued and the method of .payment under sub-section (2) of section 6;

d) the matters relating to the type of digital signature, manner and format in which it may be affixed under section 10;

e) the security procedure for the purpose of creating secure electronic record and secure digital signature under section 16;

f) the qualifications, experience and terms and conditions of service of Controller, Deputy Controllers and Assistant Controllers under section 17;

g) other standards to be observed by the Controller under clause (b) of subsection (2) of section 20;

h) the requirements which an applicant must fulfil under sub-section (2) of section 21;

i) the period of validity of licence granted under clause (a) of sub-section (3) of section 21;

j) the form in which an application for licence may be made under sub-section (1) of section 22;

k) the amount of fees payable under clause (c) of sub-section (2) of section 22;

l) such other documents which shall accompany an application for licence under clause (a) of sub-section (2) of section 22;

m) the form and the fee for renewal of a licence and the fee payable there of under section 23;

n) the form in which application for issue of a Digital Signature Certificate may be made under sub-section (1) of section 35;

o) the fee to be paid to the Certifying Authority for issue of a Digital Signature Certificate under sub-section (2) of section 35;

p) the manner in which the adjudicating officer shall hold inquiry under subsection (1) of section 46;

q) the qualification and experience which the adjudicating officer shall possess under sub-section (3) of section 46;

r) the salary, allowances and the other terms and conditions of service of the Presiding Officer under section 52;

s) the procedure for investigation of misbehaviour or incapacity of the Presiding Officer under sub-section (3) of section 54;

t) the salary and allowances and other conditions of service of other officers and employees under sub-section (3} of section 56;

u) the form in which appeal may be filed and the fee thereof under sub -section (3) of section 57;

v) any other power of a civil court required to be prescribed under clause (g) of sub-section (2) of section 58; and

w) any other matter which is required to be, or may be, prescribed.

3) Every notification made by the Central Government under clause (f) of subsection (4) of section 1 and every rule made by it shall be laid, as soon as may be after it is made, before each House of Parliament, while it is in session, for a total period of thirty days

which may be comprised in one session or in two or more successive sessions, and if, before the expiry of the session immediately following the session or the successive sessions aforesaid, both Houses agree in making any modification in the notification or the rule or both Houses agree that the notification or the rule should not be made, the notification or the rule shall thereafter have effect only in such modified form or be of no effect, as the case may be; so, however, that any such modification or annulment shall be without prejudice to the validity of anything previously done under that notification or rule.

88. Constitution of advisory committee

1) The Central Government shall, as soon as may be after the commencement of this Act, constitute a Committee called the Cyber Regulations Advisory Committee.

2) The Cyber Regulations Advisory Committee shall consist of a Chairperson and such number of other official and non-official members representing the interests principally affected or having special knowledge of the subject-matter as the Central Government may deem fit.

3) The Cyber Regulations Advisory Committee shall advise:

   a) the Central Government either generally as regards any rules or for any other purpose connected with this Act;

   b) the Controller in framing the regulations under this Act.

4) There shall be paid to the non-official members of such Committee such travelling and other allowances as the Central Government may fix.

89. Power of controller to make regulations

1) The Controller may, after consultation with the Cyber Regulations Advisory Committee and with the previous approval of the Central Government, by notification in the *Official Gazette*, make regulations consistent with this Act and the rules made thereunder to carry out the purposes of this Act.

2) In particular, and without prejudice to the generality of the foregoing power, such regulations may provide for all or any of the following matters, namely:

   a) the particulars relating to maintenance of database containing the disclosure record of every Certifying Authority under clause (m) of section 18;

   b) the conditions and restrictions subject to which the Controller may recognise any foreign Certifying Authority under sub-section (1) of section 19;

   c) the terms and conditions subject to which a licence may be granted under clause (c) of sub-section (3) of section 21;

   d) other standards to be observed by a Certifying Authority under clause (d) of section 30;

   e) the manner in which the Certifying Authority shall disclose the matters specified in sub-section (1) of section 34;

f) the particulars of statement which shall accompany an application under sub-section (3) of section 35;

g) the manner in which the subscriber shall communi-cate the compromise of private key to the certifying Authority under sub-section (2) of section 42.

3) Every regulation made under this Act shall be laid, as soon as may be after it is made, before each House of Parliament, while it is in session, for a total period of thirty days which may be comprised in one session or in two or more successive sessions, and if, before the expiry of the session immediately following the session or the successive sessions aforesaid, both Houses agree in making any modification in the regulation or both Houses agree that the regulation should not be made, the regulation shall thereafter have effect only in such modified form or he of no effect, as the case may be; so, however, that any such modification or annulment shall be without prejudice to the validity of anything previously done under that regulation.

90. Power of state government to make rules

1) The State Government may, by notification in the Official Gazette, make rules to carry out the provisions of this Act.

2) In particular, and without prejudice to the generality of the foregoing power, such rules may provide for all or any of the following matters, namely:

a) the electronic form in which filing, issue, grant receipt or payment shall be effected under sub-section (1) of section 6;

b) for matters specified in sub-section (2) of section 6;

c) any other matter which is required to be provided by rules by the State Government.

3) Every rule made by the State Government under this section shall be laid, as soon as may be after it is made, before each House of the State Legislature where it consists of two Houses, or where such Legislature consists of one House, before that House.

91. Amendment of Act 45 of 1860

The Indian Penal Code shall be amended in the manner specified in the First Schedule to this Act.

92. Amendment of Act 1 of 1872

The Indian Evidence Act, 1872 shall be amended in the manner specified in the Second Schedule to this Act.

93. Amendment of Act 18 of 1891

The Bankers' Books Evidence Act, 1891 shall be amended in the manner specified in the Third Schedule to this Act.

94. Amendment of Act 2 of 1834

The Reserve Bank of India Act, 1934 shall be amended in the manner specified in the Fourth Schedule to this Act.

THE FIRST SCHEDULE
(See section 91)

Amendments to the Indian Penal Code (45 of 1860)

After section 29, the following section shall be inserted, namely:

Electronic record

1. "29A. The words "electronic record" shall have the meaning assigned to them in clause (t) of sub-section (1) of section 2 of the Information Technology Act, 2000".
2. In section 167, for the words "such public servant, charged with the preparation or translation of any document, frames or translates that document", the words "such public servant, charged with the preparation or translation of any document or electronic record, frames, prepares or translates that document or electronic record" shall be substituted.
3. In section 172, for the words "produce a document in a Court of Justice", the words "produce a document or an electronic record in a Court of Justice" shall be substituted.
4. In section 173, for the words "to produce a document in a Court of Justice", the words "to produce a document or clectronic record in a Court of Justice" shall be substituted.
5. In section 175, for the word "document" at both the places where it occurs, the words "document or electronic record" shall be substituted.

6. In section 192, for the words "makes any false entry in any book or record, or makes any document containing a false statement", the words "makes any false entry in any book or record, or electronic record or makes any document or electronic record containing a false statement" shall be substituted.

7. In section 204, for the word "document" at both the places where it occurs, the words "document or electronic record" shall be substituted.

8. In section 463, for the words "Whoever makes any false documents or part of a document with intent to cause damage or injury", the words "Whoever makes any false documents or false electronic record or part of a document or electronic record, with intent to cause damage or injury" shall be substituted.

9. In section 464,

   a) for the portion beginning with the words "A person is said to make a false document" and ending with the words "by reason of deception practised upon him, he does not know the contents of the document or the nature of the alteration", the following shall be substituted, namely:

   "A person is said to make a false document or false electronic record:

   "First, who dishonestly or fraudulently:

   a) makes, signs, seals or executes a document or part of a document;

   b) makes or transmits any electronic record or part of any electronic record;

c) affixes any digital signature on any electronic record;

d) makes any mark denoting the execution of a document or the authenticity of the digital signature, with the intention of causing it to be believed that such document or part of document, electronic record or digital signature was made, signed, sealed, executed, transmitted or affixed by or by the authority of a person by whom or by whose authority he knows that it was not made, signed, sealed, executed or affixed; or

"Second, who, without lawful authority, dishonestly or fraudulently, by cancellation or otherwise, alters a document or an electronic record in any material part thereof, after it has been made, executed or affixed with digital signature either by himself or by any other person, whether such person be living or dead at the time of such alteration; or

"Third, who dishonestly or fraudulently causes any person to sign, seal, execute or alter a document or an electronic record or to affix his digital signature on any electronic record knowing that such person by reason of unsoundness of mind or intoxication cannot, or that by reason of deception practised upon him, he does not know the contents of the document or electronic record or the nature of the alteration."

b) after explanation 2, the following Explanation shall be inserted at the end, namely:

Explanation 3: For the purposes of this section, the expression "affixing digital signature" shall have the meaning assigned to it in clause (d) of subsection (1) of section 2 of the Information Technology Act, 2000.

10. In section 466,

a) for the words "Whoever forges a document", the words "Whoever forges a document or an electronic record" shall be substituted;

b) the following explanation shall be inserted at the end, namely:

Explanation: For the purposes of this section, "register" includes any list, data or record of any entries maintained in the electronic form as defined in clause (r) of sub-section (1) of section 2 of the Information Technology Act, 2000".

11. In section 468, for the words "document forged", the words "document or electronic record forged" shall be substituted.

12. In section 469, for the words "intending that the document forged", the words "intending that the document or electronic record forged" shall be substituted.

13. In section 470, for the word "document" in both the places where it occurs, the words "document or electronic record" shall be substituted.

14. In section 471, for the word "document" wherever it occurs, the words "document or electronic record" shall be substituted.

15. In section 474, for the portion beginning with the words "Whoever has in his possession any document" and ending with the words "if the document is one of the description mentioned in section 466 of this Code", the following shall be substituted, namely:

> "Whoever has in his possession any document or electronic record, knowing the same to be forged and intending that the same shall fraudulently or dishonestly be used as a genuine, shall, if the document or electronic record is one of the description mentioned in section 466 of this Code".

16. In section 476, for the words "any document", the words "any document or electronic record" shall be substituted.

17. In section 477A, for the words "book, paper, writing" at both the places where they occur, the words "book, electronic record, paper, writing" shall be substituted.

THE SECOND SCHEDULE

(See section 92)

Amendments to the Indian Evidence Act, 1872 (1 of 1872)

1. In section 3,

   a) in the definition of "Evidence", for the words "all documents produced for the inspection of the Court", the words "all documents including electronic records produced for the inspection of the Court" shall be substituted;

b) after the definition of "India", the following shall be inserted, namely: 'the expressions "Certifying Authority", "digital signature", "Digital Signature Certificate", "electronic form", "electronic records", "information", "secure electronic record", "secure digital signature" and "subscriber" shall have the meanings respectively assigned to them in the Information Technology Act, 2000.

2. In section 17, for the words "oral or documentary,", the words "oral or documentary or contained in electronic form" shall be substituted.

3. After section 22, the following section shall be inserted, namely:

When oral admission as to contents of electronic records are relevant.

"22A. Oral admissions as to the contents of electronic records are not relevant, unless the genuineness of the electronic record produced is in question".

4. In section 34, for the words "Entries in the books of account", the words "Entries in the books of account, including those maintained in an electronic form" shall be substituted.

5. In section 35, for the word "record", in both the places where it occurs, the words "record or an electronic record" shall be substituted.

6. For section 39, the following section shall be substituted, namely:

   What evidence to be given when statement forms part of a conversation, document, electronic record, book or series of letters or papers.

   "39. When any statement of which evidence is given forms part of a longer statement, or of a conversation or pan of an isolated document, or is contained in a document which forms part of a book, or is contained in part of electronic record or of a connected series of letters or papers, evidence shall be given of so much and no more of the statement, conversation, document, electronic record, book or series of letters or papers as the Court considers necessary in that particular case to the full understanding of the nature and effect of the statement, and of the circumstances under which it was made".

7. After section 47, the following section shall be inserted, namely:

Opinion as to digital signature where relevant.

"47A. When the Court has 10 form an opinion as to the digital signature of any person, the opinion of the Certifying Authority which has issued the Digital Signature Certificate is a relevant fact".

8. In section 59, for the words "contents of documents" the words "contents of documents or electronic records" shall be substituted.

9. After section 65, the following sections shall be inserted, namely:

Special provisions as to evidence relating to electronic record

65A. The contents of electronic records may be proved in accordance with the provisions of section 65B.

Admissibility of electronic records

65B. (1) Notwithstanding anything contained in this Act, any information contained in an electronic record which is printed on a paper, stored, recorded or copied in optical or magnetic media produced by a computer (hereinafter referred to as the computer output) shall be deemed to be also a document, if the conditions mentioned in this section are satisfied in relation to the information and computer in question and shall be admissible in any proceedings, without further proof or production of the original, as evidence of any contents of the original or of any fact stated therein of which direct evidence would be admissible.

2) The conditions referred to in sub-section (1) in respect of a computer output shall be the following, namely:

a) the computer output containing the information was produced by the computer during the period over which the computer was used regularly to store or process information for the purposes of any activities regularly carried on over that period by the person having lawful control over the use of the computer;

b) during the said period, information of the kind contained in the electronic record or of the kind from which the information so contained is derived was regularly fed into the computer in the ordinary course of the said activities;

c) throughout the material part of the said period, the computer was operating properly or, if not, then in respect of any period in which it was not operating properly or was out of operation during that part of the period, was not such as to affect the electronic record or the accuracy of its contents; and

d) the information contained in the electronic record reproduces or is derived from such information fed into the computer in the ordinary course of the said activities.

3) Where over any period, the function of storing or processing information for the purposes of any activities regularly carried on over that period as mentioned in clause (a) of sub-section (2) was regularly performed by computers, whether:

a) by a combination of computers operating over that period; or

b) by different computers operating in succession over that period; or

c) by different combinations of computers operating in succession over that period; or

d) in any other manner involving the successive operation over that period, in whatever order, of one or more computers and one or more combinations of computers, all the computers used for that purpose during that period shall be treated for the purposes of this section as constituting a single computer; and references in this section to a computer shall be construed accordingly.

4) In any proceedings where it is desired to give a statement in evidence by virtue of this section, a certificate doing any of the following things, that is to say,

a) identifying the electronic record containing the statement and describing the manner in which it was produced;

b) giving such particulars of any device involved in the production of that electronic record as may be appropriate for the purpose of showing that the electronic record was produced by a computer;

c) dealing with any of the matters to which the conditions mentioned in sub-section (2) relate, and purporting to be signed by a person occupying a responsible official position in relation to the operation of the relevant device or the management of the relevant activities (whichever is appropriate) shall be evidence of any matter stated in the certificate; and for the purposes of this sub-section it shall be sufficient for a matter to be stated to the best of the knowledge and belief of the person stating it.

5) For the purposes of this section,

a) information shall be taken to be supplied to a computer if it is supplied thereto in any appropriate form and whether it is so supplied directly or (with or without human intervention) by means of any appropriate equipment;

b) whether in the course of activities carried on by any official, information is supplied with a view to its being stored or processed for the purposes of those activities by a computer operated otherwise than in the course of those activities, that information, if duly supplied to that computer, shall be taken to be supplied to it in the course of those activities;

c) a computer output shall be taken to have been produced by a computer whether it was produced by it directly or (with or without human intervention) by means of any appropriate equipment.

Explanation: For the purposes of this section any reference to information being derived from other information shall be a reference to its being derived therefrom by calculation, comparison or any other process.

10. After section 67, the following section shall be inserted, namely:

Proof as to digital signature

"67A. Except in the case of a secure digital signature, if the digital signature of any subscriber is alleged to have been affixed to an electronic record the fact that such digital signature is the digital signature of the subscriber must be proved."

11. After section 73, the following section shall be inserted, namely:

Proof as to verification of digital signature

73A. In order to ascertain whether a digital signature is that of the person by whom it purports to have been affixed, the Court may direct

a) that person or the Controller or the Certifying Authority to produce the Digital Signature Certificate;

b) any other person to apply the public key listed in the Digital Signature Certificate and verify the digital signature purported to have been affixed by that person.

Explanation: For the purposes of this section, "Controller" means the Controller appointed under sub-section (1) of section 17 of the Information Technology Act, 2000'.

12. Presumption as to Gazettes in electronic forms

After section 81, the following section shall be inserted, namely:

"81 A. The Court shall presume the genuineness of every electronic record purporting to be the *Official Gazette*, or purporting to be electronic record directed by any law to be kept by any person, if such electronic record is kept substantially in the form required by law and is produced from proper custody".

13. Presumption as to electronic agreements.

After section 85, the following sections shall be inserted, namely:

"85A. The Court shall presume that every electronic record purporting to be an agreement containing the digital signatures of the parties was so concluded by affixing the digital signature of the parties".

Presumption as to electronic records and digital signatures

85B. (1) In any proceedings involving a secure electronic record, the Court shall presume unless contrary is proved, that the secure electronic record has not been altered since the specific point of time to which the secure status relates.

2) In any proceedings, involving secure digital signature, the Court shall presume unless the contrary is proved that:

a) the secure digital signature is affixed by subscriber with the intention of signing or approving the electronic record;

b) except in the case of a secure electronic record or a secure digital signature, nothing in this section shall create any presumption relating to authenticity and integrity of the electronic record or any digital signature.

Presumption as to digital signature certificates

"85C.The Court shall presume, unless contrary is proved, that the information listed in a Digital Signature Certificate is correct, except for information specified as subscriber information which has not been verified, if the certificate was accepted by the subscriber".

14. Presumption as to electronic messages

After section 88, the following section shall be inserted, namely:

88A. The Court may presume that an electronic message forwarded by the originator through an electronic mail server to the addressee to whom the message purports to be addressed corresponds with the message as fed into his computer for transmission; but the Court shall not make any presumption as to the person by whom such message was sent.

Explanation: For the purposes of this section, the expressions "addressee" and "originator" shall have the same meanings respectively assigned to them in clauses (b) and (za) of sub-section (1) of section 2 of the Information Technology Act, 2000.

15. Presumption as to electronic records five years old.

After section 90, the fol'owing section shall be inserted, namely:

90A. Where any electronic record, purporting or proved to be five years old, is produced from any custody which the Court in the particular case considers proper, the Court may presume that the digital signature which purports to be the digital signature of any particular person was so affixed by him or any person authorised by him in this behalf.

Explanation: Electronic records are said to be in proper custody if they are in the place in which, and under the care of the person with whom, they naturally be; but no custody is improper if it is proved to have had a legitimate origin, or the circumstances of the particular case are such as to render such an origin probable.

This Explanation applies also to section 81A".

16. For section 131, the following section shall be substituted, namely:

Production of documents or electronic records which another person, having possession, could refuse to produce.

"131. No one shall be compelled to produce documents in his possession or electronic records under his control, which any other person would be entitled to refuse to produce if they were in his possession or control, unless such last-mentioned person consents to their production".

THE THIRD SCHEDULE

(See section 93)

Amendments to the Bankers' Books Evidence Act 1891 (18 of 1891)

1. In section 2:
   a) for clause (3), the following clause shall be substituted, namely:
   (3) "bankers' books" include ledgers, day-books, cash-books, account-books and all other books used in the ordinary business of a bank whether kept in the written form or as printouts of data stored in a floppy, disc, tape or any other form of electromagnetic data storage device;
   b) for clause (8), the following clause shall be substituted, namely: (8) "certified copy" means when the books of a bank:
      a) are maintained in written form, a copy of any entry in such books together with a

certificate written; the foot of such copy that it is a true copy of such entry, that such entry is contained in one of the ordinary books of the bank and was made in the usual and ordinary course of business and that such book is still in the custody of the bank, and where the copy was obtained by a mechanical or other process which in itself ensured the accuracy of the copy, a further certificate to that effect, but where the book from which such copy was prepared has been destroyed in the usual course of the bank's business after the date on which the copy had been so prepared, a further certificate to that effect, each such certificate being dated and subscribed by the principal accountant or manager of the bank with his name and official title; and

b) consist of printouts of data stored in a floppy, disc, tape or any other electromagnetic data storage device, a printout of such entry or a copy of such printout together with such statements certified in accordance with the provisions of section 2A.

After section 2, the following section shall be inserted, namely:

Conditions in the printout.

"2A. A printout of entry or a copy of printout referred to in sub-section (8) of section 2 shall be accompanied by the following, namely:

a) a certificate to the effect that it is a printout of such entry or a copy of such printout by the principal accountant or branch manager; and

b) a certificate by a person in-charge of computer system containing a brief description of the computer system and the particulars of:

   A) the safeguards adopted by the system to ensure that data is entered or any other operation performed only by authorised persons;

   B) the safeguards adopted to prevent and detect unauthorised change of data;

   C) the safeguards available to retrieve data that is lost due to systemic failure or any other reasons;

   D) the manner in which data is transferred from the system to removable media like floppies, discs, tapes or other electromagnetic data storage devices;

   E) the mode of verification in order to ensure that data has been accurately transferred to such removable media;

   F} the mode of identification of such data storage devices;

   G) the arrangements for the storage and custody of such storage devices;

   H) the safeguards to prevent and detect any tampering with the system; and

   I) any other factor which will vouch for the integrity and accuracy of the system.

c) "a further certificate from the person in-charge of the computer system to the effect that to the best of his knowledge and belief, such computer system operated properly at the material time, he was provided with all the relevant data and the printout in question represents correctly, or is appropriately derived from, the relevant data."

THE FOURTH SCHEDULE

(See section 94)

Amendment to the Reserve Bank of India Act, 1934 (2 of 1934)

In the Reserve Bank of India Act, 1934, in section 58, in sub-section (2), after clause (p), the following clause shall be inserted, namely:

> "(pp) the regulation of fund transfer through electronic means between the banks or between the banks and other financial institutions referred to in clause (c) of section 45-1, including the laying down of the conditions subject to which banks and other financial institutions shall participate in such fund transfers, the manner of such fund transfers and the rights and obligations of the participants in such fund transfers."

Bibliography

Barnard, P., 'Cognitive Resources and the Learning of Human-Computer Dialogues', in Carroll, J. M. (ed.), *Interfacing Thought; Cognitive Aspects of Human-Computer Interaction*, Cambridge, Massachusetts, MIT Press, 1987.

Bennett, John L., 'Observations on Meeting Usability Goals for software products', *Behaviour and Information Technology*, 5, (2), 1986.

Bjorn-Anderson, N. and Numford, E. (eds)., *Information Society*, North-Holland, 1982.

Buss Martin D. J. and Lynn M. Salerno, "Common Sense and Computer Security", *Harvard Business Review*, March-April 1984.

Butler, Gathorne. *Organisation and Management*, Prentice Hall, 1986.

Computer-Based National Information Systems: Technology and Public Policy Issues, Office of Technology Assessment, US Congress, Washington, DC, 1981.

Dreyfuss Joel, "What Will Send Computers Home", *Fortune*, April 2, 1984.

Earl, Michael. *Management Strategies for Information Technology*, Prentice Hall, 1989.

"Home Shopping Network—Company Report", Hanifen, Imhoff Inc., July 20, 1994.

Johnson, David B., Andrew Myles, and Charles Perkins, "The Internet Mobile Host Protocol (IMHP)", Internet Draft, February 14, 1994.

Lane, Elizabeth S. and Summerhill, Craig A., *An Internet primer for information professionals: a basic guide to networking technology*, Westport, Meckler, 1993.

Maciuszko, Kathleen, 'A quiet revolution: community online system', *Online*, Nov. 1990, 24-32.

Marsh Peter, "A Brighter Future for the Computer Kids", *New Scientist*, August 18, 1983.

MacKinnon, D.A. *et al.*, *An Introduction to Open Systems Interconnection*, New York: Computer Science Press, 1990.

Marsden, Brian W., *Communication network protocols: OSI explained*, 3rd edn., Bromley, Chartwell-Bratt, 1991.

______________ *"Britain Advances in Computerised Factories"*, New Scientist, March 19, 1981.

______________, "Japan Plans New Generation of Computers", *New Scientist*, July 16, 1981.

Marshall Rose T, *The simple book: an introduction to management of TCP/IP internet*, London, Prentice-Hall, 1991.

______________, *The open book: a practical perspective on OSI*, Englewood Cliffs, Prentice-Hall, 1990.

McClure, Charles, *The National Research and Education Network (NREN): research and policy perspectives*, Norwood, NJ, Ablex, 1001.

Perkins Charles E. and Pravin Bhagwat, "A Mobile Networking System Based on Internet Protocol", IEEE Personal Communications, First quarter, 1994.

The Spreading Danger of Computer Crime, *Business Week*, April 20, 1981.

Weizenbaum Joseph, *Computer Power and Human Reason: From Judgement to Calculation* W. H. Freeman, San Francisco, 1976 and Penguin, Harmondsworth, England, 1984.

Wightman, D. W., 'Competitive advantage through information technology', *Journal of General Management*, vol. 12, no. 4, 1987.

Winch Graham (ed.), *Information Technology in manufacturing Processes*, Rossendale, London, 1983.

Index